KB260165

saramin

Preface

For the last few decades, EFL(English as a Foreign Language) countries have focused on teaching grammar and as a result of that, most of the EFL students have tried hard to assemble basic words into phrases and sentences. In other words, they have focused too much on the "form," not the "contents" of English. It was not that helpful in speaking English fluently.

The problem is that if someone tries to assemble words without having enough input, they can't improve at all. So rather than spending time learning grammatical rules, students need to acquire a wide variety of knowledge in the target language, English, concentrating on the contents of what they want to deliver. It means that to speak English fluently, language learners need to gain sufficient language input and the language input needs to be one step beyond their current level of English ability, according to Dr. Stephen Krashen, a noted linguist.

In this series of books, I targeted at teaching English naturally by helping students acquire English speaking skills through various content-based activities.

Jiyeon Lee

Table of Contents

Unit Description

Step 1 Word Pronunciation

Word Pronunciation provides the words students need to learn to speak about the topic. It will enable students to build a relevant and comprehensive vocabulary.

Step 2 Describe Two Pictures

Describe Two Pictures offers an opportunity for students to make complete sentences by filling in blanks with suitable words to describe pictures that depict situations relating to the unit topic.

Step 3 Situational Conversation

In **Situational Conversation**, students will listen to a conversation related to the unit topic and answer three relevant questions. They will learn how to make a short conversation before going on to make a short speech.

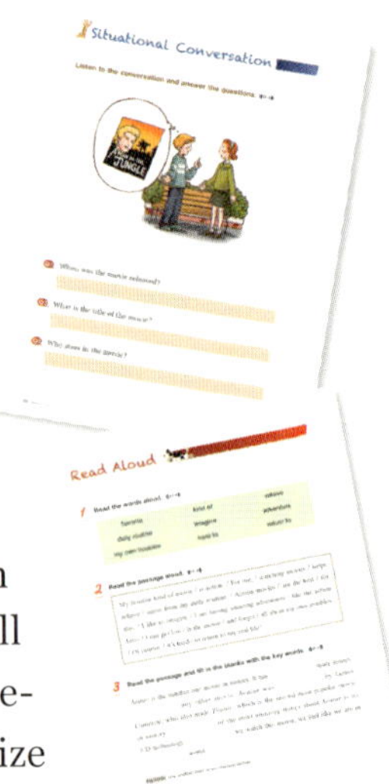

Step 4 Read Aloud

Read Aloud is designed to make students immerse themselves in English sentence structure and vocabulary by reading passages aloud repeatedly. It will eventually prepare students to be able to speak using their own words. By re-reading and memorizing the passage, students will learn how to logically organize their thoughts in English, use relevant vocabulary, and structure their speaking naturally.

In **Respond to Questions,** students will be given ten frequently asked questions relating to the unit topic. They will learn the basic patterns to answer those questions.

The last section of the unit provides an opportunity for students to consolidate the basic structures and vocabulary they have learned to talk about their own experiences and express their opinions.

Chapter 01

Theater

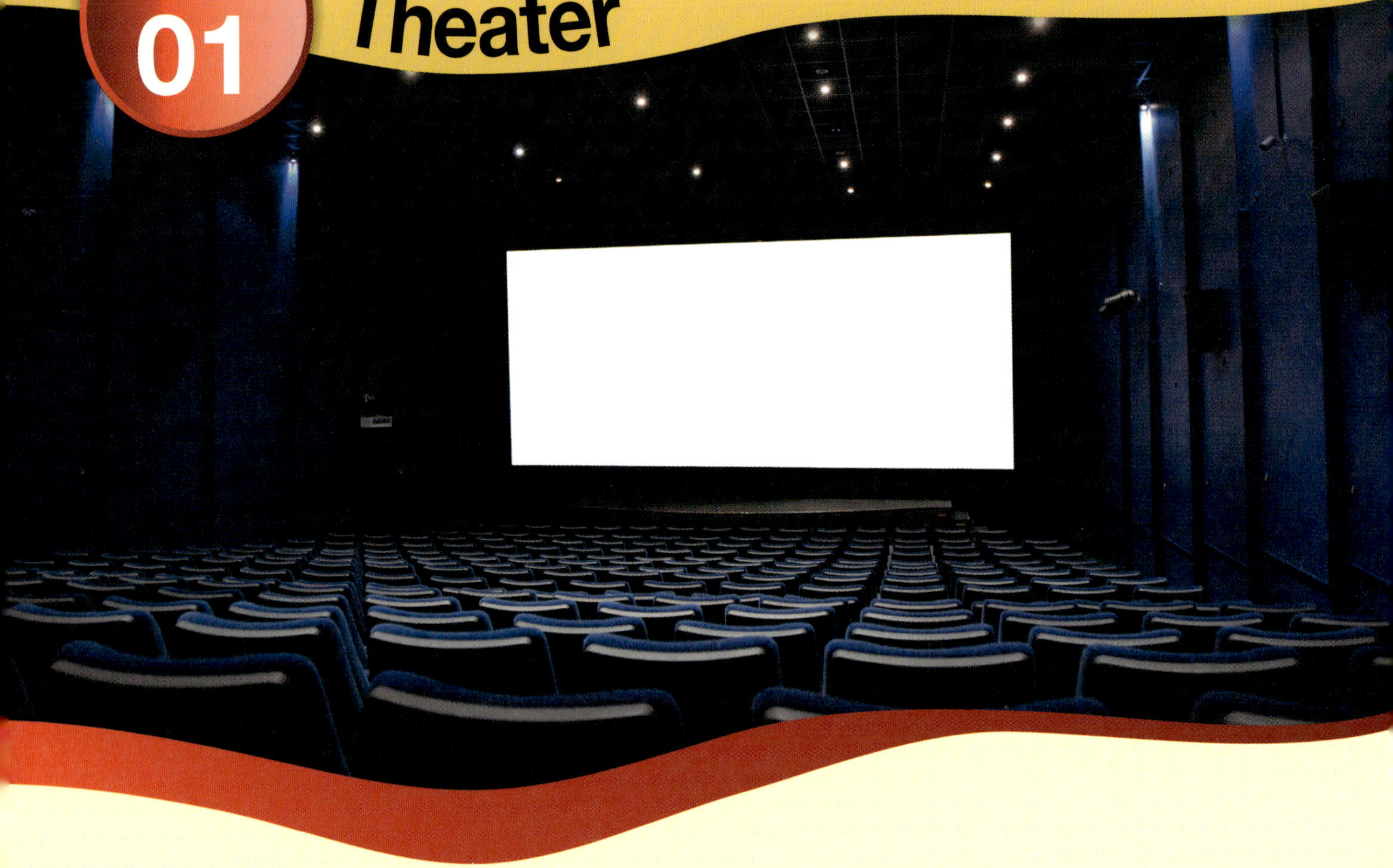

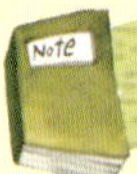

Word Pronunciation

Listen to the following words and repeat them. 01-1

- box office *n.* ____________
- actress [ǽktris] *n.* ____________
- star [stáːr] *v.* ____________
- seat [síːt] *n.* ____________
- ticket [tíkit] *n.* ____________
- direct [dirékt] *v.* ____________
- 3-D *n.* ____________
- moving [múːviŋ] *a.* ____________
- movie [múːvi] *n.* ____________
- actor [ǽktər] *n.* ____________
- popcorn [pápkɔ̀ːrn] *n.* ____________
- hero [híːərou] *n.* ____________
- release [rilíːs] *v.* ____________
- action [ǽkʃən] *n.* ____________
- title [táitl] *n.* ____________

Describe Two Pictures 

Look at the pictures and fill in the blanks with the most suitable words. 01-2

1

A man and a woman are ____________ the movie ____________.

2

An old woman is buying a movie ____________ at the ____________ office.

Listen to the conversation and answer the questions.

Q1 When was the movie released?

Q2 What is the title of the movie?

Q3 Who stars in the movie?

Read Aloud

1 **Read the words aloud.** (01-4)

favorite	kind of	relieve
daily routine	imagine	adventure
my own troubles	hard to	return to

2 **Read the passage aloud.** (01-4)

My favorite kind of movie / is action. / For me, / watching movies / helps relieve / stress from my daily routine. / Action movies / are the best / for this. / I like to imagine / I am having amazing adventures / like the action hero. / I can get lost / in the movie / and forget / all about my own troubles. / Of course, / it's hard / to return to my real life!

3 **Read the passage and fill in the blanks with the key words.** (01-4)

Avatar is the number one movie in history. It has ____________ more money ____________ any other movie. *Avatar* was ____________ by James Cameron, who also made *Titanic*, which is the second-most popular movie in history. ____________ of the most amazing things about *Avatar* is its 3-D technology. ____________ we watch this movie, we feel like we are in ____________ world.

Key Words one/ another/ than/ when/ directed/ earned

Respond to Questions

Respond to the following questions. (01-5)

Q1 What is your favorite kind of movie?
A1   I like _______________________ .

Q2 Where do you like to sit in the movie theater?
A2   I prefer to have a seat _______________________ .

Q3 What was the last movie you saw?
A3   The last movie I saw was _______________________ .

Q4 Who is your favorite actor?
A4   My favorite actor is _______________________ .

Q5 What is the worst movie you have ever seen?
A5   The worst movie I've seen was _______________________ .

Q6 What do you usually eat at the movie theater?
A6   I like _______________________ .

Q7 Who do you like to watch movies with?
A7   I prefer watching movies with _______________________ .

Q8 What do you think is a fair price for a movie ticket?
A8   I think movies should be _______________________ .

Q9 What's more important: the actors or the story?
A9   _______________________ is more important than _______________________ .

Q10 If your life was a movie, what kind of movie would it be?
A10   My movie would be a _______________________ .

Personal Experience & Opinion

Read the question and write your own answer. (01-6)

Question   What was the most moving movie you've ever watched?

Sample Answer

There was one movie I saw that really moved me a lot. It was called "*Dust Kickers.*" The movie was about a group of children who came from a poor neighborhood. The kids made a soccer team. They were really good, but they couldn't afford uniforms or good shoes. They entered a tournament and finally they won! Many people laughed at them, but they didn't care what people thought about them. The story was excellent and the actors were funny.

My Answer

- The most moving movie I've ever ____________ was " ____________ ".
- The movie was about ____________.
- My favorite part of the movie is ____________.
- I think " ____________ " is the best movie in the cinematic history.

More Questions

1 Do you like watching movies in the theater or at home?

2 What is your favorite animated movie?

3 Who is the most famous actor in your country?

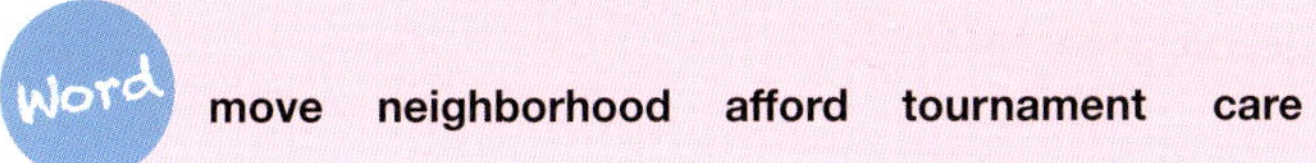

Word   move   neighborhood   afford   tournament   care

Chapter 02 Library

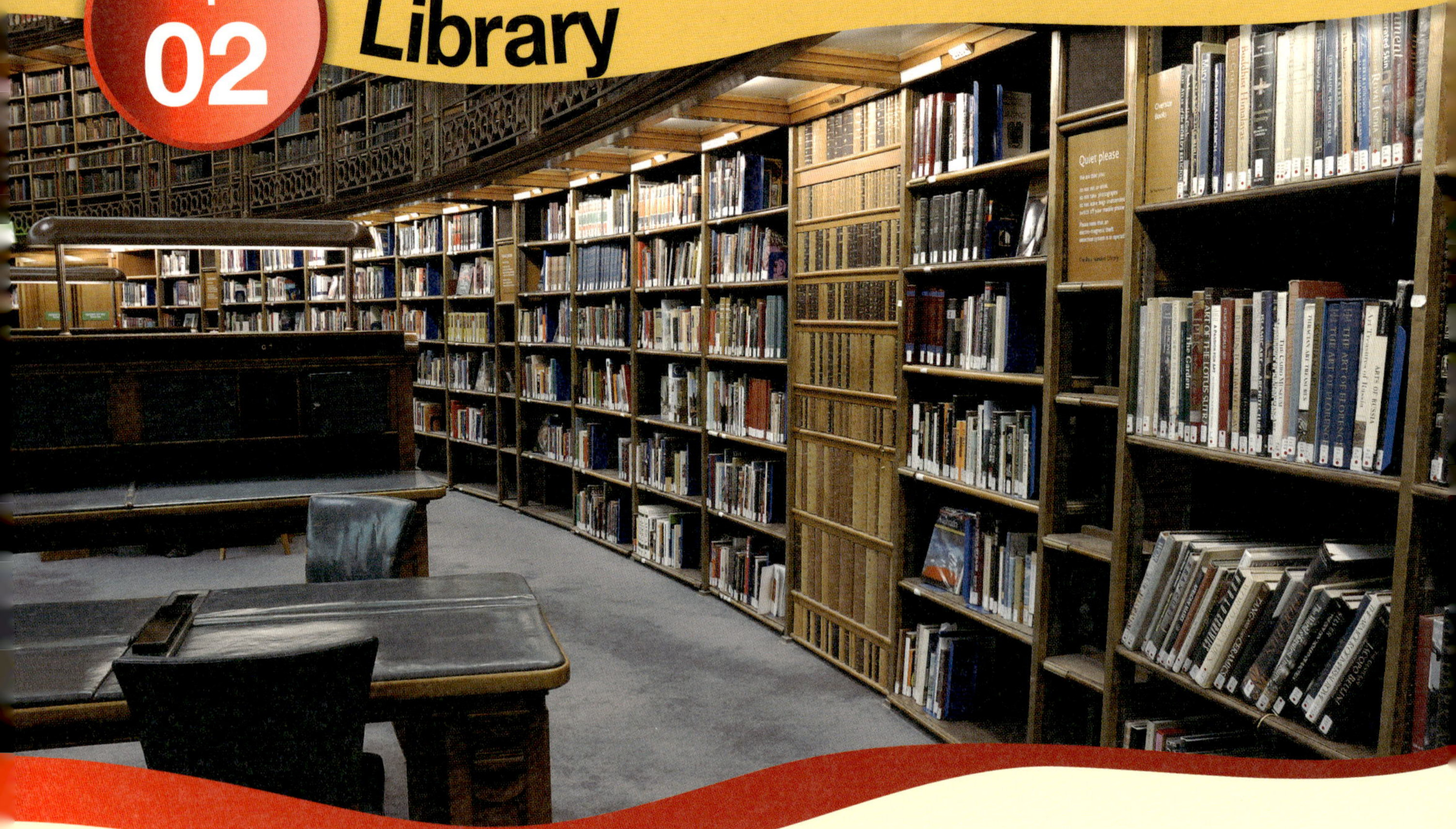

Word Pronunciation

Listen to the following words and repeat them. 02-1

- ☐ **sign out** *v.* ____________
- ☐ **return** [ritə́ːrn] *v.* ____________
- ☐ **photocopier** [fóutoukɑ́piər] *n.* ____________
- ☐ **bookshelf** [búkʃelf] *n.* ____________
- ☐ **section** [sékʃən] *n.* ____________
- ☐ **floor** [flɔ́ːr] *n.* ____________
- ☐ **writer** [ráitər] *n.* ____________
- ☐ **non-fiction** *n.* ____________
- ☐ **take out** *v.* ____________
- ☐ **take back** *v.* ____________
- ☐ **library card** *n.* ____________
- ☐ **quiet** [kwáiət] *a.* ____________
- ☐ **librarian** [laibrɛ́ːəriən] *n.* ____________
- ☐ **information** [ìnfərméiʃən] *n.* ____________
- ☐ **rule** [rúːl] *n.* ____________
- ☐ **science fiction** *n.* ____________

Describe Two Pictures

Look at the pictures and fill in the blanks with the most suitable words. (02-2)

1

A girl is signing a book out of the ______________.

2

A man is looking at books on a ______________.

Situational Conversation

Listen to the conversation and answer the questions. (02-3)

Q1 What kind of book is the man looking for?

Q2 What is on the second floor?

Q3 What do you need to take out books?

Read Aloud

1 **Read the words aloud.** (02-4)

important	shouldn't	disturb
hurt	attract	third
out of	without	wonder

2 **Read the passage aloud.** (02-4)

Libraries / have some important rules. / First, / we must be quiet. / People in the library / are studying or reading. / We shouldn't / disturb them. / Second, / we should not / eat or drink / in the library. / Food and drinks / can hurt books / and attract insects. / Third, / we should not take books / out of the library / without signing them out.

3 **Read the passage and fill in the blanks with the key words.** (02-4)

In my family, Sunday is "library day." Every Sunday we all go to the library ______________ . We have to ______________ our books ______________ and get some new ones. My mother usually goes to the kids ______________ with my little brother. My father goes to the ______________ ______________ section to read. I go to a ______________ section every week. I just like to look around and read many different things.

Key Words   section/ take/ different/ back/ magazine/ together/ newspaper/ and

Respond to Questions

Respond to the following questions. (02-5)

Q1 What kind of books do you like?

A1 I like ___________________________.

Q2 How often do you go to the library?

A2 I go to the library ___________________ a week.

Q3 What do you like to do in the library?

A3 I like to sit in the window and ___________________.

Q4 Who is your favorite writer?

A4 I like ___________________.

Q5 Who works in a library?

A5 ___________________ work in a library.

Q6 Besides books, what can you find in a library?

A6 We can find ___________________.

Q7 What happens if you don't return your books on time?

A7 I have to ___________________.

Q8 How many books do you think you read in a year?

A8 I read about ___________________ books each year.

Q9 When did you learn to read?

A9 I learned to read when I was ___________________ years old.

Q10 Do you like stories or non-fiction?

A10 I like ___________________.

Personal Experience & Opinion

Read the question and write your own answer. 02-6

Question   What was the best book you've ever read?

The best book I've ever read was *Harry Potter and the Philosopher's Stone*. It is so amazing. The story is about a young boy who goes to a magic school. He makes many friends and a few enemies. A bad wizard named Voldemort killed Harry's parents and tried to kill Harry too. Harry and his friends have to fight the wizard.

My Answer

- The best book I've ever ___________ was " ___________________________ ".
- The story was about ____ .
- My favorite character from the story is _______________________ .
- I think " ___________ " is worth ___________ because it's _______________ .

More Questions

1   What's better for finding information, the library or the Internet?

2   Describe the library that you use.

3   What is a popular book in your country right now?

Word   enemy   wizard   fight

Chapter 03 Pharmacy

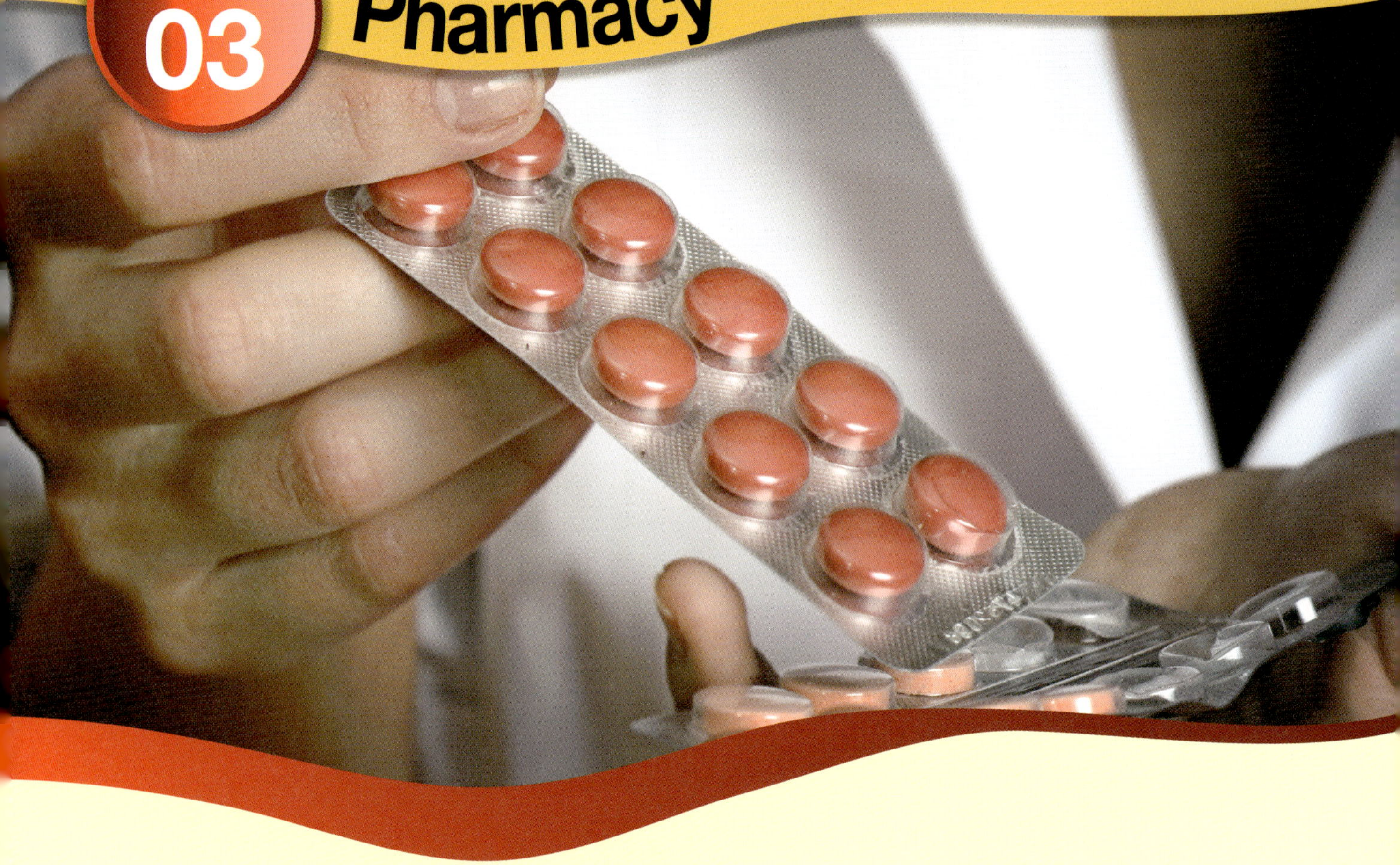

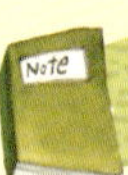

Word Pronunciation

Listen to the following words and repeat them. 03-1

- □ **pill** [píl] *n.* ______
- □ **pharmacist** [fá:rməsist] *n.* ______
- □ **liquid** [líkwid] *n.* ______
- □ **prescription** [priskrípʃən] *n.* ______
- □ **sleepy** [slí:pi] *a.* ______
- □ **sick** [sík] *a.* ______
- □ **lab coat** *n.* ______
- □ **anti-inflammatory** *n.* ______
- □ **bottle** [bátl] *n.* ______
- □ **pain** [péin] *n.* ______
- □ **medicine** [médəsin] *n.* ______
- □ **side effect** *n.* ______
- □ **chemistry** [kéməstri] *n.* ______
- □ **hurt** [hə́:rt] *v.* ______
- □ **dose** [dóus] *n.* ______

Describe Two Pictures

Look at the pictures and fill in the blanks with the most suitable words. ▌03-2▐

1

A _____________ is counting some _____________ .

2

A woman is looking at some bottles on a _____________ .

Situational Conversation

Listen to the conversation and answer the questions. 03-3

Q1 What does the person need medicine for?

Q2 What type of medicine does the pharmacist recommend?

Q3 How much does it cost?

Read Aloud

1 **Read the words aloud.** (03-4)

medicine	pharmacist	prescription
a piece of paper	what we need	only for
handwriting	usually	difficult

2 **Read the passage aloud.** (03-4)

We buy medicine / from a pharmacist. / To get some medicines, / we need a prescription. / A prescription / is a piece of paper / from the doctor / that tells the pharmacist / what we need. / The doctor writes it / on a special piece of paper / only for writing prescriptions. / Many doctors / have bad handwriting. / It is usually difficult / for the pharmacist / to read!

3 **Read the passage and fill in the blanks with the key words.** (03-4)

Pharmacists have to understand the side effects of different medicines. Side effects are the things that the medicine does that _____________ be bad. For example, maybe some medicines take away your _____________ but they make you sleepy. _____________ is a side effect. Sometimes the side effects are _____________ than your first problem! It really _____________ on the person. Different people might _____________ different side effects.

Key Words   pain/ depends/ experience/ sleepiness/ worse/ might

Respond to Questions

Respond to the following questions. (03-5)

Q1 Do you take medicine every day?

A1 No, I ________________________ need medicine every day.

Q2 Do you think medicine is expensive?

A2 Yes, medicine is very ________________________!

Q3 What subject do you think pharmacists have to be good at?

A3 They need to be good at ________________________.

Q4 Who usually goes to the pharmacy?

A4 People who are ________________________ go to the pharmacy.

Q5 Do you take medicine when you have a cold?

A5 No, I just eat ________________________ and rest.

Q6 What type of clothes does a pharmacist wear?

A6 They usually wear ________________________.

Q7 What is the DOSE on a pill bottle?

A7 The dose is how much we should ________________________.

Q8 What can you buy besides medicine in the pharmacy?

A8 We can buy ________________________.

Q9 How far is the closest pharmacy to your house?

A9 The closest pharmacy is ________________________ away.

Q10 In what other places can we find a pharmacy?

A10 We can see pharmacies in ________________________.

Personal Experience & Opinion

Read the question and write your own answer. 〔03-6〕

Question Have you ever had to take medicine that tasted bad?

Sample Answer

Yes! I was sick once with a bad stomach problem. The doctor examined me and told me I had to take some medicine. I went with my mother to the pharmacy to buy it. It was a dark brown thick liquid. I had to drink it three times every day. It tasted really bad. I almost couldn't swallow it.

My Answer

- I was sick once with ________________________.
- I went to ________________________.
- The doctor prescribed me ________________________.
- It was ____________ and tasted ________________________.

More Questions

1 Do you think you would like to be a pharmacist?

2 How has a pharmacist helped you before?

3 Describe the inside of a pharmacy near your home.

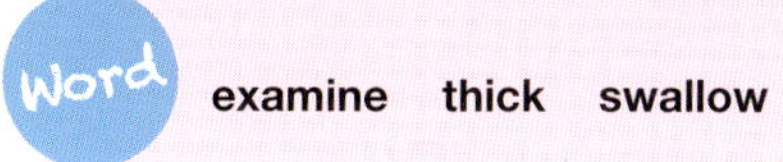

Word examine   thick   swallow

Chapter 04 Restaurant

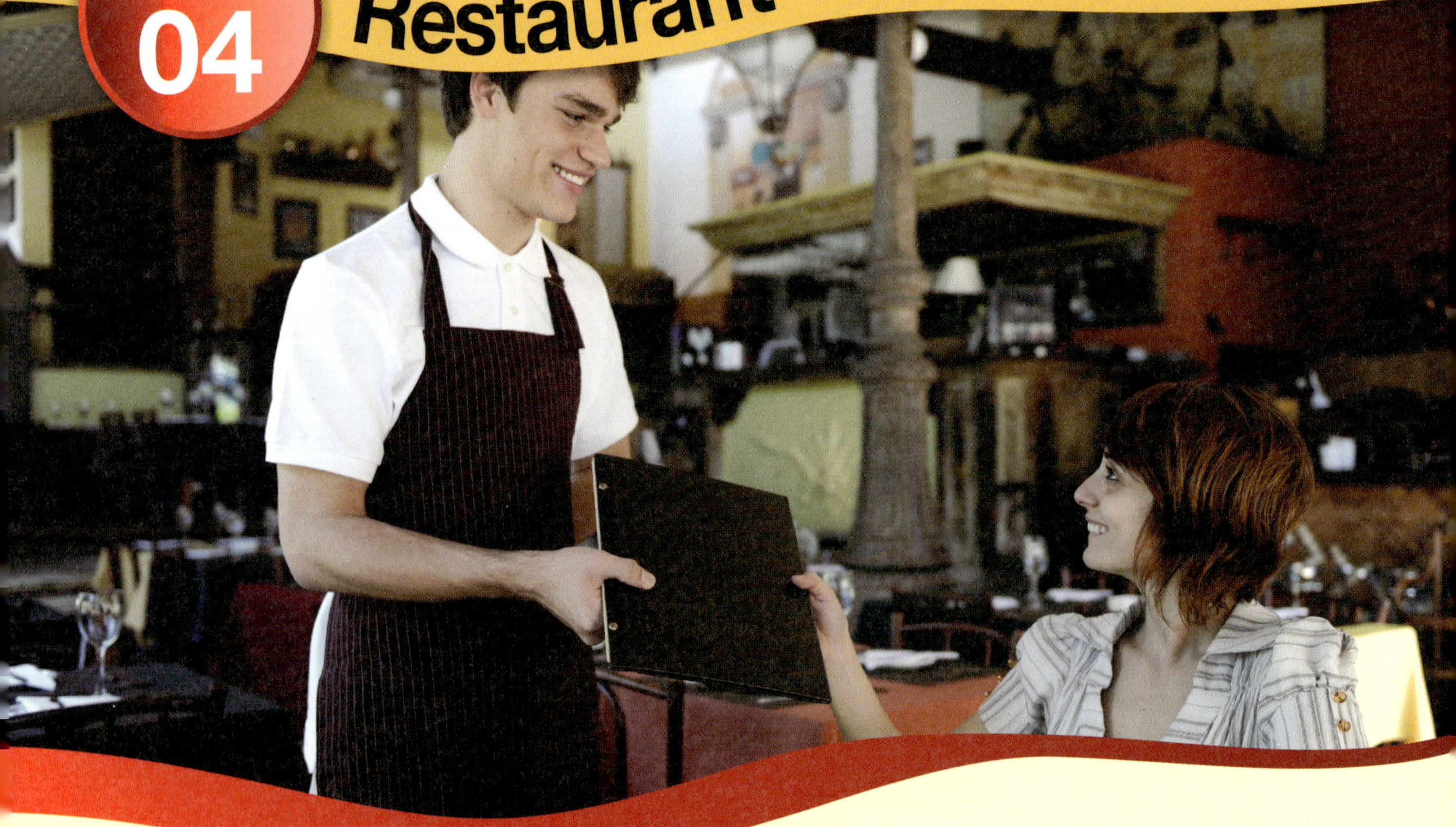

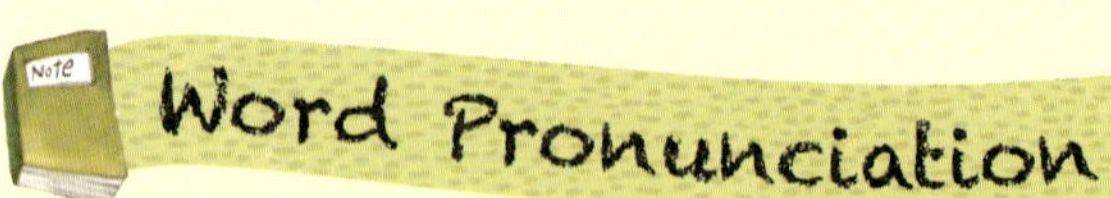

Word Pronunciation

Listen to the following words and repeat them. 04-1

- □ **menu** [ménjuː] *n.* ______
- □ **chicken** [tʃíkən] *n.* ______
- □ **customer** [kʌ́stəmər] *n.* ______
- □ **supper** [sʌ́pər] *n.* ______
- □ **cook** [kúk] *v.* ______
- □ **fast food** *n.* ______
- □ **bill** [bíl] *n.* ______
- □ **amount** [əmáunt] *n.* ______
- □ **table** [téibl] *n.* ______
- □ **order** [ɔ́ːrdər] *n.* ______
- □ **waiter** [wéitər] *n.* ______
- □ **go out** *v.* ______
- □ **taste** [téist] *n.* ______
- □ **pay** [péi] *v.* ______
- □ **expensive** [ikspénsiv] *a.* ______

Describe Two Pictures 

Look at the pictures and fill in the blanks with the most suitable words.
(04-2)

1

A waiter is giving the ______________ to a customer at a ______________ .

2

A man and a woman are ______________ in a ______________ .

Situational Conversation

Listen to the conversation and answer the questions. ❙ 04-3 ❙

Q1 What does the man order?

Q2 What will the man have with it?

Q3 What will the man drink?

Read Aloud

1 Read the words aloud. (04-4)

eat out	end	feel like
kind of	try	different countries
many things	each other	look forward to

2 Read the passage aloud. (04-4)

My family / eats out / every Friday evening. / It is the end of the week / and my mother / doesn't feel like cooking. / We / go to a different kind of restaurant / every week. / It's fun / to try food / from different countries. / We always order / many things / and try each other's food. / All week / I look forward to supper / on Friday, / though my mom / is a good cook.

3 Read the passage and fill in the blanks with the key words. (04-4)

Being a waiter is a difficult job. You have to always be very nice to ____________. You have to make sure everyone has exactly what they want or need. When the restaurant is ____________, you can't take a break. There's always something to do. Sometimes customers are very demanding. This can make the job very ____________.

Key Words stressful/ customer/ busy/ every

Respond to Questions

Respond to the following questions. (04-5)

Q1 How often do you eat in a restaurant?

A1 About _________________________ times per week.

Q2 What is your favorite kind of food?

A2 I really like _______________ food, especially _______________ .

Q3 What is your favorite restaurant?

A3 My favorite restaurant is called _________________________ .

Q4 Who has the most difficult job in a restaurant?

A4 _________________________ has the most difficult job.

Q5 What's more important, the taste or the amount of food?

A5 I think _________________________ is more important.

Q6 What kind of fast food do you like?

A6 I like _________________________ .

Q7 Who pays when you go out for supper?

A7 _________________________ always pays.

Q8 Does your city have a good variety of restaurants?

A8 No. I wish we had _________________________ .

Q9 What's the strangest food you've eaten in a restaurant?

A9 I ate _________________________ .

Q10 What's your favorite lunch food?

A10 I like _________________________ .

Personal Experience & Opinion

Read the question and write your own answer. (04-6)

 What's the worst restaurant experience you've had?

Sample Answer

One time I went for lunch with my dad. We went to a really good soup place. I ordered my favorite mushroom soup, but when it came I found a cockroach in it. I screamed and my dad complained. They brought me a different kind of soup but I wasn't hungry anymore. I tried to eat but I just felt sick. My dad refused to pay the bill.

My Answer

- One day, I went to a ____________ for ____________________ .
- I ordered ____ .
- When they brought it, I found ____________________________ .
- I tried to eat, but ____________________________ .

More Questions

1 What's the best restaurant meal you've ever had?

2 What's the most expensive restaurant you've been to?

3 What kind of food haven't you tried but would like to?

Word cockroach   scream   complain   anymore   refuse

Home

Word Pronunciation

Listen to the following words and repeat them. (05-1)

☐ **kitchen** [kítʃən] *n.* ___________________

☐ **house** [háus] *n.* ___________________

☐ **bedroom** [bédrùːm] *n.* ___________________

☐ **dining room** *n.* ___________________

☐ **comfortable** [kʌ́mfərtəbl] *a.* ___________________

☐ **homesick** [hóumsìk] *a.* ___________________

☐ **guest** [gést] *n.* ___________________

☐ **neighbor** [néibər] *n.* ___________________

☐ **basement** [béismənt] *n.* ___________________

☐ **attic** [ǽtik] *n.* ___________________

☐ **family** [fǽməli] *n.* ___________________

☐ **living room** *n.* ___________________

☐ **bathroom** [bǽθrùːm] *n.* ___________________

☐ **location** [loukéiʃən] *n.* ___________________

☐ **roommate** [rúːmmèit] *n.* ___________________

Describe Two Pictures 

Look at the pictures and fill in the blanks with the most suitable words. 05-2

1

A man is washing ______________ in the ______________ .

2

A family is ______________ TV together on the ______________ .

Situational Conversation

Listen to the conversation and answer the questions. 05-3

Q1 Why didn't the boy walk the dog?

Q2 When will the boy walk the dog?

Q3 What is the dog's name?

Read Aloud

1   Read the words aloud. (05-4)

dream about	swimming pool	tennis court
backyard	bedroom	enough
two dozen	would need	clean

2   Read the passage aloud. (05-4)

Sometimes / I dream about / living in a large house. / It has a swimming pool / in the basement, / a tennis court / in the backyard, / and my bedroom is / in the attic. / It has enough rooms / for all my family and friends / and a large kitchen / with a dining room / big enough / for two dozen people. / All I would need / is someone / to clean it / for me.

3   Read the passage and fill in the blanks with the key words. (05-4)

Home is my favorite place in the world. My home is not just my house, but also my family's and the place we do ______________ ______________. It is ______________ and ______________. Sometimes when we go away on a ______________, I think about how nice it will be to come home. I ______________ my bedroom and just ______________ ______________ with my brothers and sisters in the living room.

Key Words   hanging/ together/ out/ vacation/ comfortable/ safe/ everything/ miss

Respond to Questions

Respond to the following questions. 🔊 05-5

Q1 What kind of home do you live in?

A1 I live in ______________________________.

Q2 How many times have you moved in your life?

A2 I have moved ______________ times.

Q3 What's your favorite room in your house?

A3 I like ______________________.

Q4 How many bathrooms are in your house?

A4 There are ______________ bathrooms in my house.

Q5 Would you rather live in the country or city?

A5 I prefer to live in ______________.

Q6 How often do you have guests in your home?

A6 We have guests ______________.

Q7 What is the best location for a home?

A7 The best location is near ______________.

Q8 How well do you know your neighbors?

A8 I know my neighbors ______________.

Q9 What is an important quality in a roommate?

A9 A roommate should be ______________.

Q10 What is your house made of?

A10 My house is made of ______________.

Personal Experience & Opinion

Read the question and write your own answer. (05-6)

Question   When was a time that you were homesick?

Sample Answer

Last summer I went to camp for one month. It was fun, but I really missed my home and my family. I had terrible homesickness. We could only use the telephone once a week. It was hard not to talk to my parents every day. I even missed fighting with my brother. It's good to feel homesickness, I think, because it makes me realize how much I love my family.

My Answer

- Last ______________, I went to ________________ for ______________.
- It was ______________ but I ____________________________.
- I missed even ____.
- Being homesick makes me ________________________.

More Questions

1   Have you ever been scared in your house alone?

2   Describe your house.

3   If you could change one thing about your house, what would you change?

Word   miss   realize

Chapter 06 Clothing Store

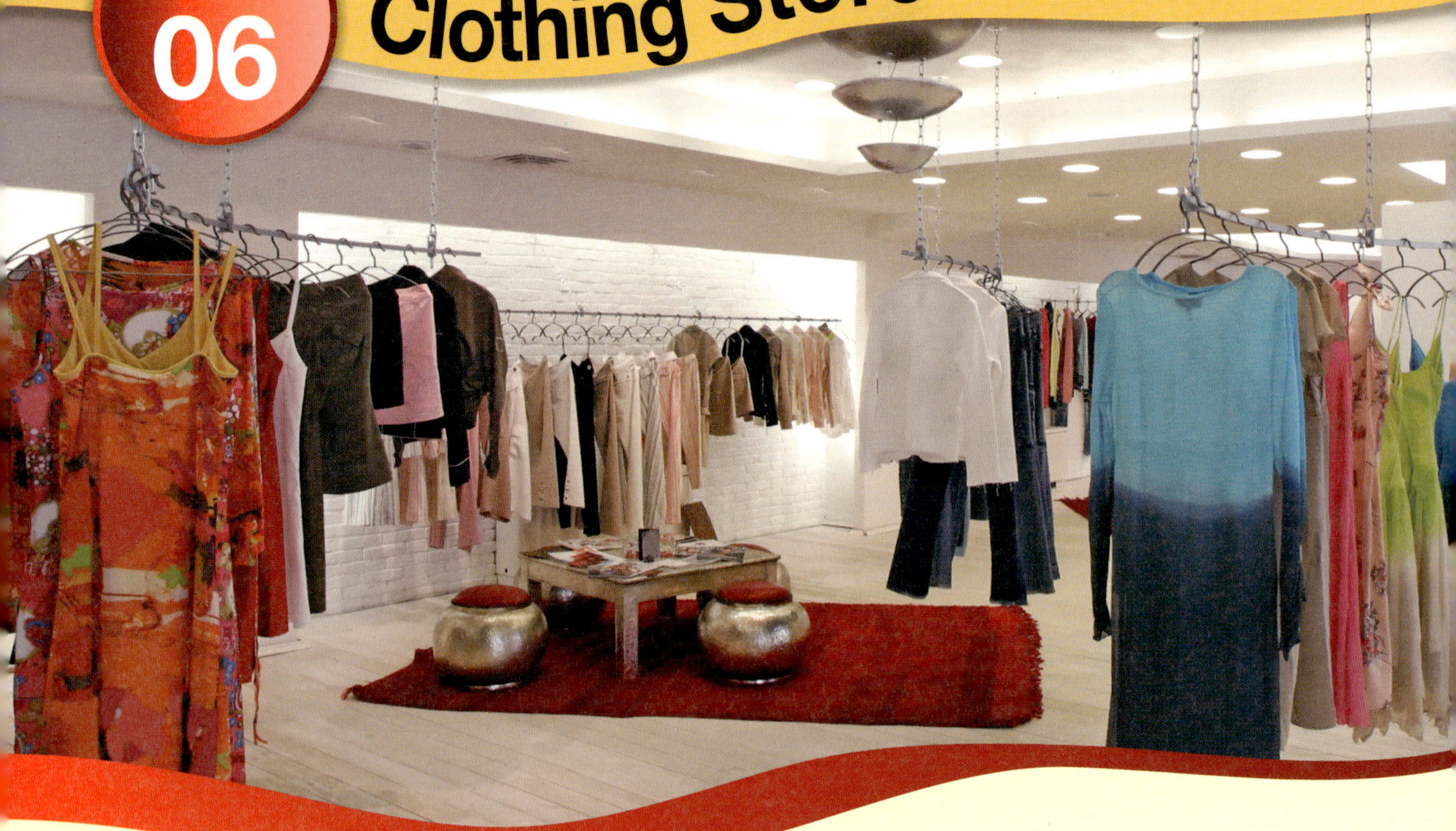

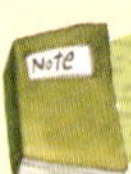

Word Pronunciation

Listen to the following words and repeat them. 06-1

- **try on** *v.* ______
- **shelf** [ʃélf] *n.* ______
- **storeroom** [stɔ:ru:m] *n.* ______
- **picky** [píki] *a.* ______
- **credit card** *n.* ______
- **fashion** [fǽʃən] *n.* ______
- **browse** [bráuz] *v.* ______
- **dress up** *v.* ______
- **size** [sáiz] *n.* ______
- **fit** [fít] *v.* ______
- **on sale** *a.* ______
- **clerk** [klə:rk] *n.* ______
- **style** [stáil] *n.* ______
- **trend** [trénd] *n.* ______
- **shopping** [ʃápiŋ] *n.* ______

Look at the pictures and fill in the blanks with the most suitable words. ❚06-2❚

1

A woman is trying ___________ a ___________ for size.

2

Two boys are looking at ___________ on a ___________ .

Listen to the conversation and answer the questions. (06-3)

Q1 What's wrong with the shirt?

Q2 What size does the man need?

Q3 What is on sale?

Read Aloud

1 Read the words aloud. (06-4)

clothing store	picky about	clothes
ugly	complain	different ideas
argue	feel bad	go alone

2 Read the passage aloud. (06-4)

My mother / doesn't like / going to the clothing store / with me. / I'm very picky / about clothes. / She wants me / to try on things / that I think are ugly. / I complain / a lot. / We have / very different ideas / about fashion. / We often argue / in the store. / I feel bad / for the clerk / who has to help us! / I just wish / my mother / would give me her credit card / and let me go alone.

3 Read the passage and fill in the blanks with the key words. (06-4)

I like shopping! I can spend all day at the _____________ going to different clothing stores. When I _____________ _____________, I want to _____________ my own clothing store. I will have all the _____________ styles and people can come to my store to find out what the newest trends are. It won't be too expensive, so that everybody can look good _____________ they don't have much money.

Key Words   mall/ even/ if/ run/ grow/ up/ latest

Respond to Questions

Respond to the following questions. (06-5)

Q1 How often do you buy clothes?

A1   I buy clothes about _________________________ .

Q2 Do you like to browse without buying?

A2   No. I think browsing is _________________________ .

Q3 What is your favorite color for clothing?

A3   I prefer _________________________ .

Q4 Do you think fashion is important?

A4   I like it, but it's _________________________ .

Q5 Do you think new clothes are too expensive?

A5   It depends on _________________________ .

Q6 What's your favorite clothing store?

A6   I really like _________________________ .

Q7 Do you ever buy second-hand clothes?

A7   _________________________ .

Q8 What items do you spend the most money on?

A8   I spend the most on _________________________ .

Q9 Do you prefer summer or winter clothes?

A9   I like _________________________ .

Q10 How often do you get dressed up?

A10   I get dressed up about _________________________ .

Personal Experience & Opinion

Read the question and write your own answer. (06-6)

Question   What was the most expensive piece of clothing you've ever bought?

Sample Answer

The most expensive piece of clothing I've ever bought was a coat. It was a big blue wool winter coat with beautiful buttons. I really wanted it and asked my mother every day to buy it for me. Finally, just before Christmas my mother took me to the store. She told me to try one on. I was so surprised. When we found the right size, she bought it. I was so happy.

My Answer

- The most expensive piece of clothing I've ever bought is ______________ ".
- It was ______________ .
- I really wanted it, so ______________ .
- When I bought it, I ______________ .

More Questions

1   Where did you go on your last shopping trip?

2   If you had $200 to spend on clothes, what would you buy?

3   What is a bad experience you have had in a clothing store?

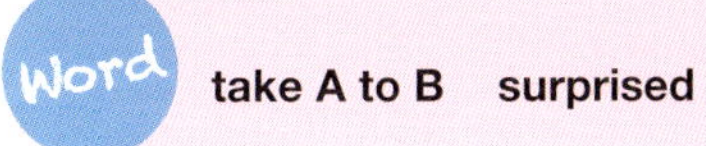

Word   take A to B   surprised

Chapter 07

Supermarket

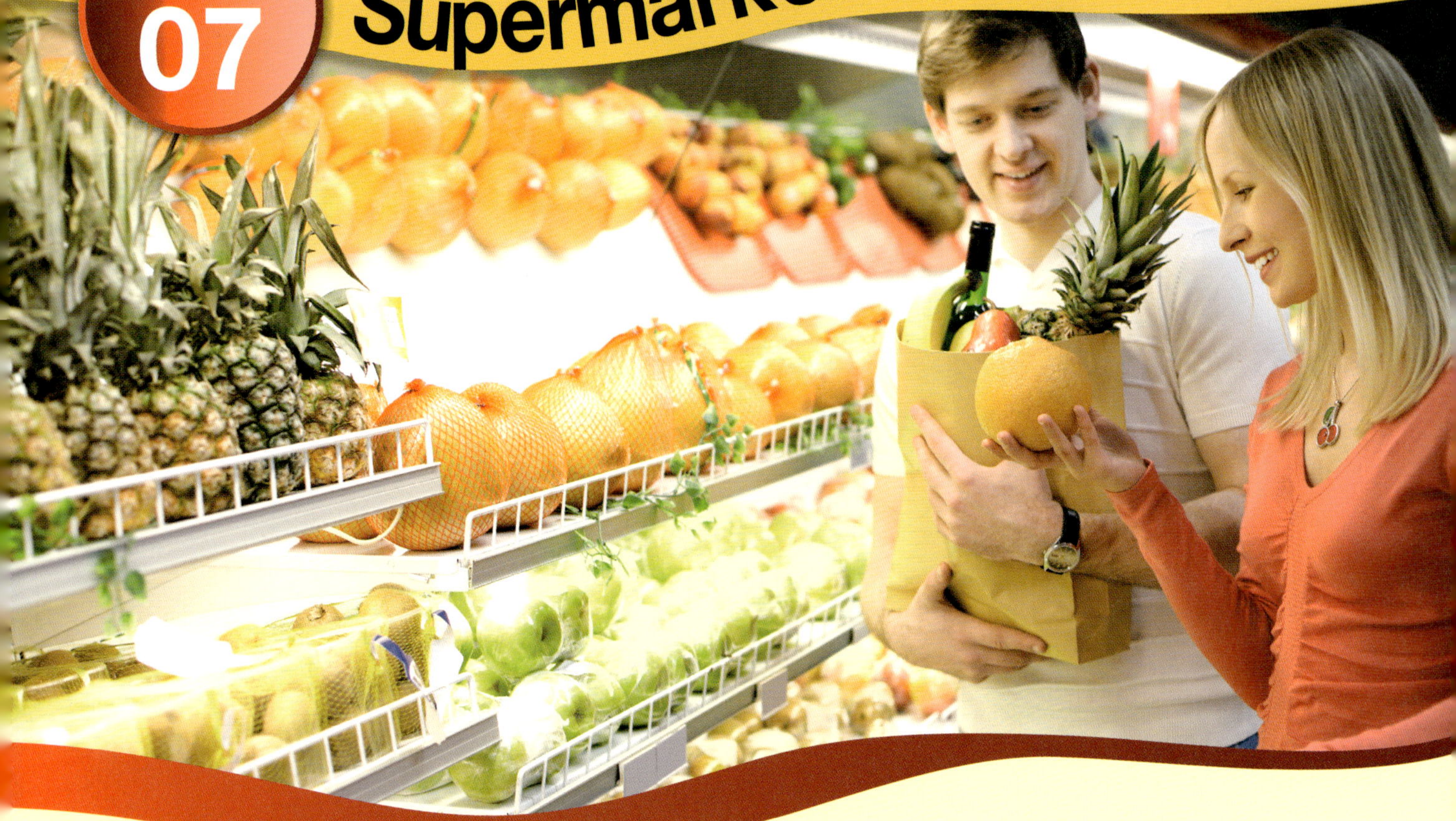

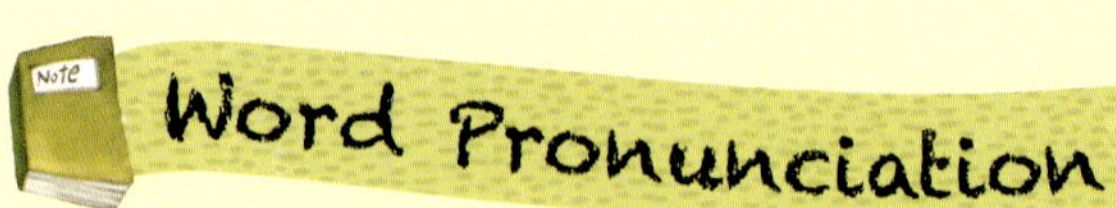

Word Pronunciation

Listen to the following words and repeat them. 07-1

□ **cashier** [kæʃíər] *n.* ________	□ **customer** [kʌ́stəmər] *n.* ________
□ **aisle** [áil] *n.* ________	□ **sale** [séil] *n.* ________
□ **produce** [prədjúːs] *v.* ________	□ **meat** [míːt] *n.* ________
□ **dairy** [dɛ́ːəri] *n.* ________	□ **frozen** [fróuzən] *a.* ________
□ **bulk** [bʌ́lk] *n.* ________	□ **list** [líst] *n.* ________
□ **grocery** [gróusəri] *n.* ________	□ **jar** [dʒáːr] *n.* ________
□ **can** [kən] *n.* ________	□ **section** [sékʃən] *n.* ________
□ **shopping cart** *n.* ________	

Describe Two Pictures

Look at the pictures and fill in the blanks with the most suitable words. 07-2

1

A ______________ is taking money from a ______________ .

2

A woman is ______________ at different kinds of ______________ .

Situational Conversation

Listen to the conversation and answer the questions. 07-3

Q1 What is the man looking for?

Q2 Where is it located?

Q3 What is on sale?

Read Aloud

1 **Read the words aloud.** (07-4)

supermarket	produce section	fruits and vegetables
dairy section	cheese	milk
yoghurt	frozen food	bulk section

2 **Read the passage aloud.** (07-4)

The supermarket / has many different sections. / In the produce section, / we can find / fruits and vegetables. / In the dairy section / we can buy / cheese, milk, yoghurt and eggs. / The meat section / contains meat, / of course. / Frozen foods / have their own special place, / and some supermarkets / have a bulk section, / where you can buy / different foods / by weight.

3 **Read the passage and fill in the blanks with the key words.** (07-4)

When you go to the supermarket, it is a good idea to __________ __________ __________ of what you need first. Then you can __________ __________ things on the list. If you don't have a list, then you might __________ some things. Then when you __________ home you __________ the things you should have bought. Without a list, it is also easier to buy things you don't __________ !

Key Words   remember/ forget/ list/ for/ a/ look/ make/ get/ need

Respond to Questions

Respond to the following questions. (07-5)

Q1 In your family, who usually buys groceries?

A1 _________________________ usually buys the groceries.

Q2 What kinds of foods are most expensive at the supermarket?

A2 _________________ is the most expensive.

Q3 What is something that you usually buy in a jar?

A3 We usually buy _________________ in a jar.

Q4 What is something that you usually buy in a can?

A4 We buy _________________________ in a can.

Q5 What is a shopping cart?

A5 A shopping cart helps us _____________ our groceries through the store.

Q6 Does your family buy all the groceries at one store?

A6 No, we buy _________________________ at different stores.

Q7 How often does your family go to the supermarket?

A7 We go _________________________ .

Q8 What is your favorite section of the supermarket?

A8 I like _________________________ .

Q9 What is something your family often buys frozen?

A9 We often buy _________________________ .

Q10 If you had $20 to spend at the supermarket, what would you buy?

A10 I'd buy _________________________ .

Personal Experience & Opinion

Read the question and write your own answer. ❙07-6❙

Question If you wanted to make your favorite meal, what would you need to buy from the grocery store?

Sample Answer

My favorite meal is spaghetti, so the first thing I need is spaghetti. Then I need to make sauce, so I need to buy tomatoes, onions, garlic and mushrooms. With spaghetti, it's very nice to have good bread, so I need to buy that too. Finally, I think it would be good to have a simple salad, so I would buy lettuce, cucumber, and radishes.

My Answer

- My favorite meal is _______________, so the first thing I need _____________.
- Then I need ______________________________________.
- It's very nice to have ______________________________with it.
- Finally, it would be good to have ___________, so I would buy ___________.

More Questions

1 What do you think should be improved in your local grocery store?

2 What is your worst supermarket experience?

3 When you go to the supermarket, what special things do you like to buy?

Word sauce garlic lettuce cucumber radish

Chapter 08

Hospital

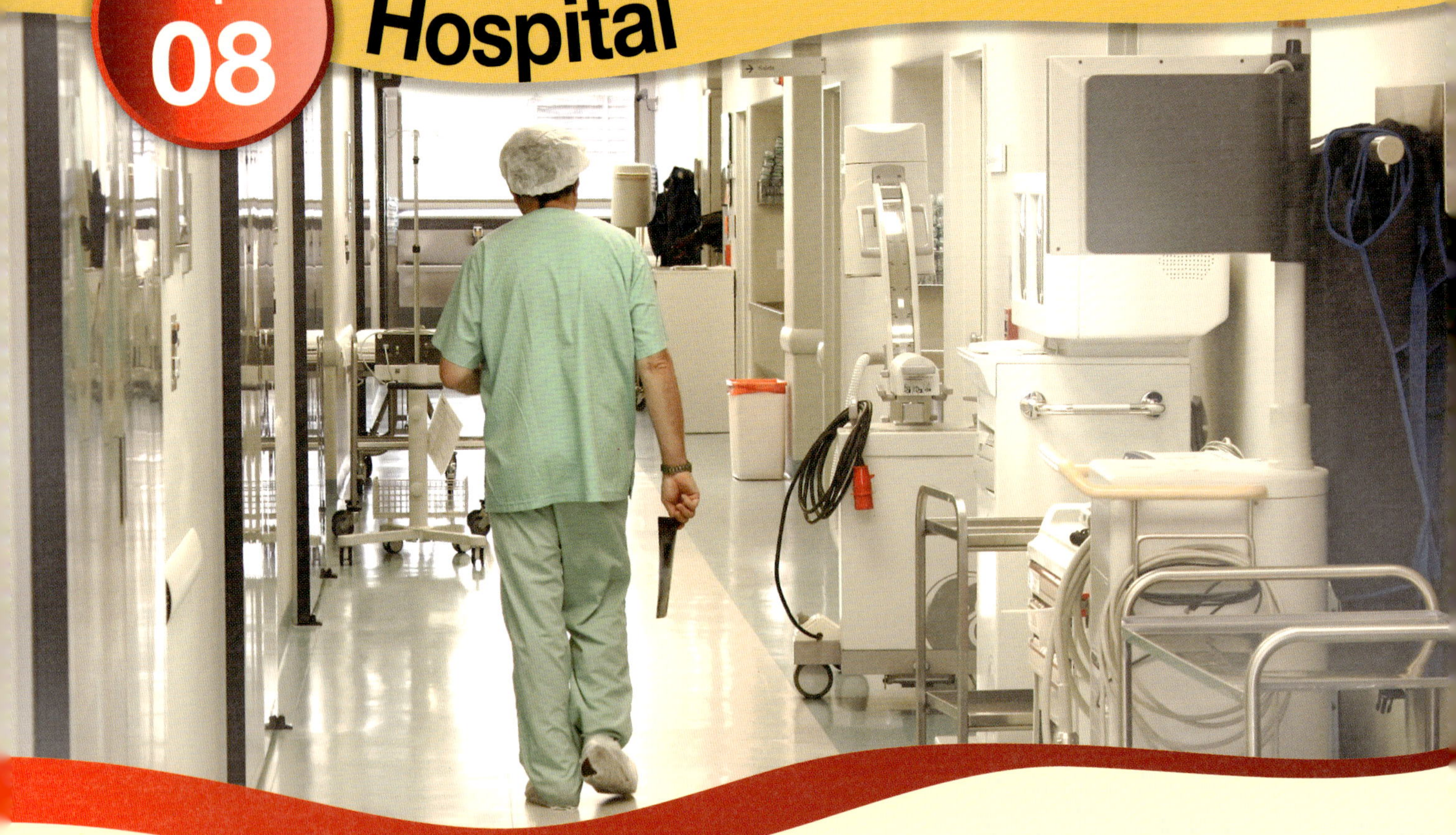

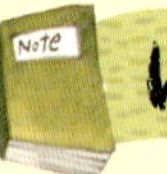

Word Pronunciation

Listen to the following words and repeat them. 08-1

- **patient** [péiʃənt] *n.* ____________
- **emergency** [imə́:rdʒənsi] *n.* ____________
- **sick** [sík] *a.* ____________
- **surgery** [sə́:rdʒəri] *n.* ____________
- **surgeon** [sə́:rdʒən] *n.* ____________
- **needle** [ní:dl] *n.* ____________
- **x-ray** *n.* ____________
- **car accident** *n.* ____________
- **doctor** [dáktər] *n.* ____________
- **visiting hours** *n.* ____________
- **hurt** [hə́:rt] *v.* ____________
- **cancer** [kǽnsər] *n.* ____________
- **broken** [bróukən] *a.* ____________
- **ambulance** [ǽmbjələns] *n.* ____________
- **cast** [kǽst] *n.* ____________

Describe Two Pictures

Look at the pictures and fill in the blanks with the most suitable words. (08-2)

1

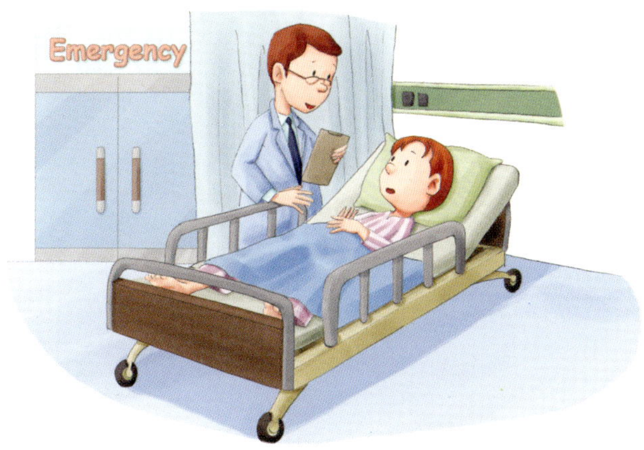

A doctor is talking to a ______________ in the ______________ ward.

2

A family is gathered ______________ a patient's ______________.

Q1 What room is the patient in?

Q2 What time are visiting hours?

Q3 What must you do before going into the room?

Read Aloud

1 Read the words aloud. 08-4

one of	injured	section
for children	pregnant women	many others
specialized	which means	for only

2 Read the passage aloud. 08-4

A hospital is/one of the most important buildings / in any town or city. / This is the place / we go / if we are sick / or injured. / In a hospital / there are / different sections. / There is a part / for children, / a part / for emergencies, / a part / for pregnant women, / a part / for old people, / and many others. / Some hospitals / are specialized, / which means / they are / for only one thing, / like babies.

3 Read the passage and fill in the blanks with the key words. 08-4

The operating room is one of ________________ ________________ ________________ places in the hospital. This is where doctors do surgery. Surgery means going inside the body to ________________ or remove something. If you have a ________________ leg, you might need surgery to fix it. If you have ________________ , you might need surgery ________________ ________________ it. A doctor who does surgery ________________ ________________ a surgeon.

Key Words remove/ the/ cancer/ called/ broken/ is/ interesting/ most/ to/ fix

Respond to Questions

Respond to the following questions. (08-5)

Q1 What color do doctors usually wear?

A1 They usually wear ________________________.

Q2 Have you ever been to a hospital?

A2 Yes, I have been ________________________ times.

Q3 Have you ever broken a bone?

A3 Yes, I broke ________________________.

Q4 Why do doctors wash their hands a lot?

A4 They don't want to ________________________.

Q5 Are you afraid of needles?

A5 Yes, I hate ________________________.

Q6 What is a good reason to go the hospital?

A6 If you have ________________________.

Q7 What is a poor reason to go to the hospital?

A7 When you have ________________________.

Q8 How do you feel when you are in a hospital?

A8 I feel ________________________.

Q9 What kind of personality should a nurse have?

A9 A nurse should be ________________________.

Q10 What's the fastest way to get to the hospital?

A10 ________________________.

Personal Experience & Opinion

Read the question and write your own answer. (08-6)

Question Talk about a time that you were in a hospital.

> ### Sample Answer
>
> One time I fell off my bicycle and broke my arm. It hurt a lot. My mother drove me to the hospital. Some kind nurses helped me onto a bed. I had to wait a long time to see a doctor. The hospital was very busy that day. Finally the doctor examined me. He took x-rays of my arm. Then he put a cast on my arm. The cast was hard and stopped me from moving my arm.

My Answer

- One time I ________________________________ .
- Some ________________ helped me ________________ .
- The hospital was ________________ that day.
- The doctor examined and ________________ .

More Questions

1 What kind of questions does a doctor ask first when you go to the hospital?

2 What is a good gift to take to someone in the hospital?

3 Do you prefer to have a male or female doctor?

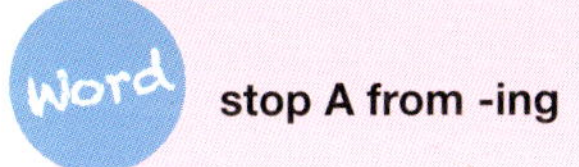

Word   **stop A from -ing**

Chapter 09

Subway

Word Pronunciation

Listen to the following words and repeat them. (09-1)

- **platform** [plǽtfɔːrm] *n.* ___________
- **stop** [stáp] *n.* ___________
- **exit** [égzit] *n.* ___________
- **crowded** [kráudid] *a.* ___________
- **system** [sístəm] *n.* ___________
- **passenger** [pǽsəndʒər] *n.* ___________
- **catch** [kǽtʃ] *v.* ___________
- **arrive** [əráiv] *v.* ___________

- **train** [tréin] *n.* ___________
- **station** [stéiʃən] *n.* ___________
- **rush hour** *n.* ___________
- **seat** [síːt] *n.* ___________
- **line** [láin] *n.* ___________
- **ride** [ráid] *v.* ___________
- **stair** [stɛər] *n.* ___________

Describe Two Pictures

Look at the pictures and fill in the blanks with the most suitable words. 09-2

1

Many people are _____________ on the _____________.

2

A person is _____________ a _____________ on the train.

Listen to the conversation and answer the questions. (09-3)

Q1 What is the next stop?

Q2 What is located there?

Q3 Which exit should the person take?

Read Aloud

1 Read the words aloud. 09-4

at rush hour	go to work	in the evening
at that time	subway	crowded
get a seat	usually	hot and smelly

2 Read the passage aloud. 09-4

The subway / is very busy / at rush hour. / Rush hour / is the time / when many people are going to work / or coming home / from work. / This usually means / from 7:00 to 9:00 / in the morning / and 5:00 to 7:00 / in the evening. / At that time, / the subway / is very crowded. / It is difficult / to get a seat. / It is also / usually very hot and smelly.

3 Read the passage and fill in the blanks with the key words. 09-4

The London Underground is a very _______________ subway system. It was first built _____________ 150 years ago, which means it is _______________ _______________ subway in the world. The London Underground is sometimes called the "Tube." It has 275 _______________ along 12 lines. The lines have different names and different colors on the _______________ . Every day, the London Underground _____________ about 3 million passengers.

Key Words the/ famous/ oldest/ carries/ stations/ map/ over

Respond to Questions

Respond to the following questions. (09-5)

Q1 Do you like riding the subway?

A1 ____

Q2 What is the best thing about the subway?

A2 It _______________________________________ .

Q3 What is the worst thing about the subway?

A3 Sometimes it is _____________________________ .

Q4 How often do you use the subway?

A4 I use it ___________________________________ .

Q5 Do you think the subway is dangerous?

A5 No, because ________________________________ .

Q6 What do you think when people talk on cell phones on the subway?

A6 I really don't like that because ___________________ .

Q7 What do you usually do when you are on the subway?

A7 I usually read a book or _____________________ .

Q8 Do you ever give your seat to someone else?

A8 Yes. I give my seat to ______________________ .

Q9 Have you ever lost something on the subway?

A9 Yes, I lost _________________________ on the subway.

Q10 How do you feel when the train is late?

A10 I feel ____________________________________ .

Personal Experience & Opinion

Read the question and write your own answer. (09-6)

Question   What is the worst experience you have had on the subway?

Sample Answer

I had a very bad experience on the subway last year. I was hurrying because I got up late. I had to catch the subway to school. I ran down the stairs to the platform. The train was just arriving. I had to run really fast to get on before the doors closed. I made it, but my shoe came off on the platform! I had to go to school with just one shoe.

My Answer

- I had my worst experience on the subway ___________________________ .
- I was hurrying because ___________________________ .
- The train I need to catch was ___________________________ .
- I had to ___________________________ .

More Questions

1   How can your city make the subway better?

2   What is the nicest subway station you have seen?

3   What should you be careful about when you ride the subway?

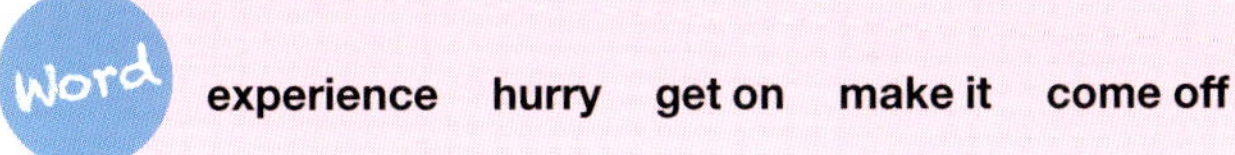

Taxi

Word Pronunciation

Listen to the following words and repeat them. (10-1)

☐ **license** [láisəns] *n.* _______	☐ **catch** [kǽtʃ] *v.* _______
☐ **accident** [ǽksidənt] *n.* _______	☐ **tip** [típ] *n.* _______
☐ **back seat** *n.* _______	☐ **front seat** *n.* _______
☐ **wave** [wéiv] *v.* _______	☐ **expensive** [ikspénsiv] *a.* _______
☐ **meter** [mí:tər] *n.* _______	☐ **fare** [fɛər] *n.* _______
☐ **traffic** [trǽfik] *n.* _______	☐ **hail** [héil] *v.* _______
☐ **transportation** [trὰnspərtéiʃən] *n.* _______	☐ **street** [strí:t] *n.* _______
☐ **address** [ədrés] *n.* _______	

Look at the pictures and fill in the blanks with the most suitable words. ◖10-2◗

1

A woman is trying to _______________ a taxi in the street.

2

A taxi driver is talking to a person in the _______________.

Situational Conversation

Listen to the conversation and answer the questions. (10-3)

Q1 Where is the passenger going?

Q2 Why will it take half an hour?

Q3 What does the passenger want the driver to do?

Read Aloud

1 **Read the words aloud.** (10-4)

not easy	all its streets	address
get there	stress	because of
late at night	deal with	get tips

2 **Read the passage aloud.** (10-4)

Being a taxi driver / is not easy. / You need to know / the city / and all its streets / very well. / If someone / gives you an address, / you have to know / exactly how to get there. / Drivers / have stress too / because of traffic. / Sometimes / they have to work late / at night / and sometimes / they have to deal with / difficult passengers. / One good thing / is that / sometimes they get tips.

3 **Read the passage and fill in the blanks with the key words.** (10-4)

Taking a taxi is more expensive than _____________ _____________ _____________ transportation. The taxi has a special meter that _____________ the cost. The meter starts at a basic price. Then it _____________ up as the taxi drives. _____________ _____________ you go, the higher the fare. This is not _____________ the bus or subway, where you pay one price to travel in a certain area.

Key Words like/ the/ other/ kinds/ of/ shows/ farther/ goes

Respond to Questions

Respond to the following questions. (10-5)

Q1 How often do you take a taxi?

A1 ______________________________ .

Q2 Have you ever taken a taxi alone?

A2 ______________________________ .

Q3 What color are taxis in your city?

A3 Taxis in my city are ____________________ .

Q4 When is it most difficult to catch a taxi?

A4 Usually ________________________ it is difficult.

Q5 How do you make a taxi stop?

A5 I ________________________ my hand.

Q6 Is it better to sit in the front or the back seat?

A6 I prefer ________________________ .

Q7 Do taxi drivers need a special licence?

A7 Yes, they need ______________________ .

Q8 In your city, do people tip taxi drivers?

A8 ______________________________ .

Q9 What do taxi drivers usually like to talk about?

A9 They usually talk about ____________________ .

Q10 Do you think taxis are expensive?

A10 ______________________________ .

Personal Experience & Opinion

Read the question and write your own answer. (10-6)

Question   What is the worst taxi experience you've had?

Sample Answer

One time my father and I were going to a concert. Our taxi had an accident with another taxi. It wasn't too serious, but the drivers were very angry. They shouted at each other in the street. We were worried about being late, so we got out. My father paid the man, but he was angry that we were leaving. We had to catch a different taxi.

My Answer

- One time I was going to ________________________________.
- I got in the taxi, and the driver was ________________________________.
- I was __________ about ________________________________.
- I had to ________________________________.

More Questions

1 What should you be careful about when taking a taxi?

2 Do you think there are enough taxis in your city?

3 Besides driving, what do taxi drivers do as part of their job?

Word   shout   careful

Chapter 11 Bus

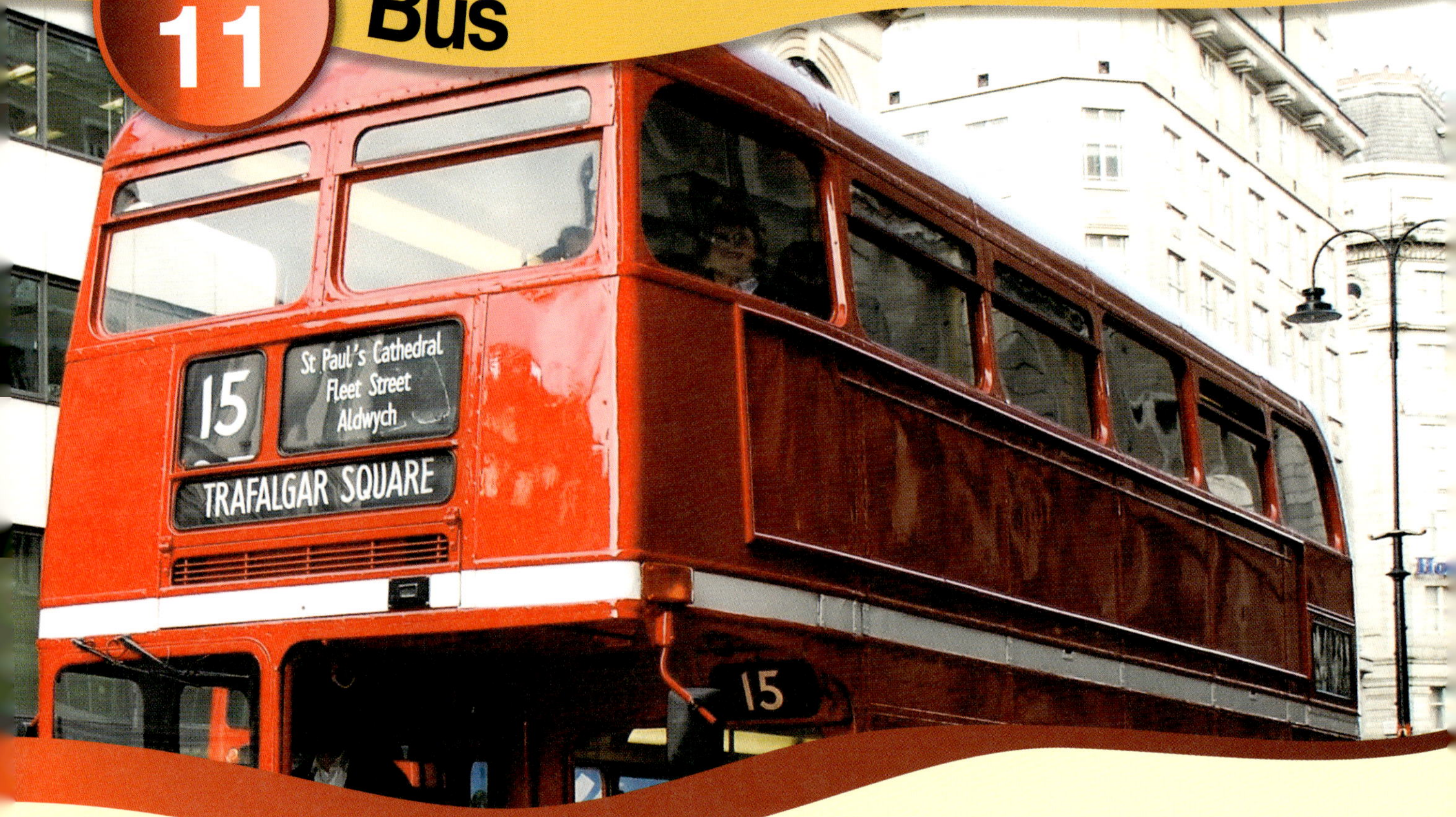

Word Pronunciation

Listen to the following words and repeat them. 11-1

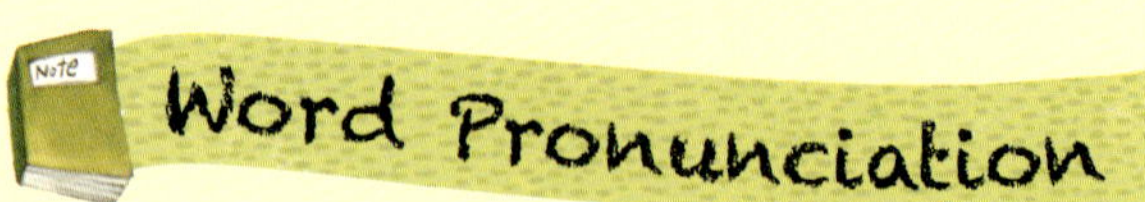

- □ **fare** [fɛər] *n.* ______________
- □ **coin** [kɔ́in] *n.* ______________
- □ **fare box** *n.* ______________
- □ **route** [rúːt] *n.* ______________
- □ **stop** [stάp] *n.* ______________
- □ **cord** [kɔ́ːrd] *n.* ______________
- □ **transfer** [trǽnsfər] *v.* ______________
- □ **seat** [síːt] *n.* ______________
- □ **downtown** [dàuntáun] *n.* ______________
- □ **transportation** [trӕnspərtéiʃən] *n.* ______________
- □ **number** [nʌ́mbər] *n.* ______________
- □ **station** [stéiʃən] *n.* ______________
- □ **take** [téik] *v.* ______________
- □ **bell** [bél] *n.* ______________
- □ **schedule** [skédʒuːl] *n.* ______________

Describe Two Pictures

Look at the pictures and fill in the blanks with the most suitable words. (11-2)

1

Several people are ________________ at a bus ________________ .

2

A woman is putting ________________ into the ________________ box.

Q1 Where is the woman going?

Q2 How much is the adult fare?

Q3 How many children does the woman have?

Read Aloud

1 **Read the words aloud.** (11-4)

public transportation	every city	bus system
route	have to	then
find	bus stop	wait for

2 **Read the passage aloud.** (11-4)

Buses are / one very important part / of public transportation. / Every city / has a bus system / for its people. / Every bus / has a number / and a route. / The route / is / where the bus goes. / To use the bus system, / you need to know / which route and number / you have to take. / Then / you can find / the bus stop / and wait / for that bus.

3 **Read the passage and fill in the blanks with the key words.** (11-4)

A bus station is for buses that travel between towns _____________ _____________. At the bus station, you can see all sort of people. Some of them are waiting to catch a bus to _____________ _____________. Others are waiting for someone to arrive on a bus. These buses transport _____________ _____________ people but also _____________ and other mail. This is a cheap way to send something to someone.

Key Words only/ cities/ packages/ and/ place/ not/ another

Respond to Questions

Respond to the following questions. (11-5)

Q1 Do you like taking the bus?

A1 Yes, I think ___________________________ .

Q2 How often do you take the bus?

A2 I take the bus _________________________ .

Q3 How old were you when you first took the bus alone?

A3 I was ___________________________ old.

Q4 Where do you like to sit on the bus?

A4 I like to sit ________________________ .

Q5 What do you usually do on a long bus ride?

A5 I _____________________________ .

Q6 If you want the bus to stop, what do you have to do?

A6 I have to _______________________ .

Q7 What's the longest bus trip you've ever taken?

A7 I took a _____________ bus ride to ______________ one time.

Q8 Why is the bus better than the subway?

A8 Because ________________________ .

Q9 What kind of personality should a bus driver have?

A9 A bus driver should be __________________ .

Q10 What do you need if you want to change buses?

A10 I need _________________________ .

Personal Experience & Opinion

Read the question and write your own answer. (11-6)

Question   What is the worst thing about taking the bus?

Sample Answer

The worst thing about taking a bus is that sometimes I have to wait. I hate waiting. I always look at the schedule to see when the bus runs, but it almost never arrives at the right time. And the longer I have to wait, the more people gather. That means the bus is really crowded and I can't find a seat.

My Answer

- The worst thing about taking a bus is _________________________________.
- I hate _________________________________.
- The longer I have to wait, _________________________________.
- That means _________________________________.

More Questions

1   How do you want your city to improve the buses?

2   What's the best long-distance bus trip you have taken?

3   What's better, the subway or the bus?

Word   hate   gather   improve   distance

Chapter 12

Shoe Store

Word Pronunciation

Listen to the following words and repeat them. (12-1)

- **display** [displéi] *v.* _______________
- **try on** *v.* _______________
- **athletic shoes** *n.* _______________
- **pair** [pɛər] *n.* _______________
- **sneakers** [sníːkərs] *n.* _______________
- **sandals** [sǽndəls] *n.* _______________
- **boots** [búːts] *n.* _______________
- **worn out** *a.* _______________

- **high heels** *n.* _______________
- **size** [sáiz] *n.* _______________
- **cleat** [klíːt] *n.* _______________
- **comfort** [kʌ́mfərt] *n.* _______________
- **dress shoes** *n.* _______________
- **flip-flop** [flípflàp] *n.* _______________
- **slippers** [slípərs] *n.* _______________

Describe Two Pictures 

Look at the pictures and fill in the blanks with the most suitable words. (12-2)

1

A man is looking through a ______________ at a ____________ display.

2

A woman is trying on a ____________ of high ____________ .

Listen to the conversation and answer the questions. (12-3)

Q1 What is the woman going to do?

Q2 What color does the woman want?

Q3 What size is the woman's feet?

Read Aloud

1 Read the words aloud. (12-4)

shoe sizes	confusing	go shopping
for example	wear	in Europe
in England	in Korea	the whole world

2 Read the passage aloud. (12-4)

Shoe sizes / are different / in different places. / It can be / very confusing / if you go shopping / in another country. / For example, / if you are a woman / and wear a size 35 / in Europe, / then / you need a 21 / in Japan, / a 2.5 / in England, / a 5 / in America / and a 228 / in Korea. / Somebody should make / one system / that the whole world / can use.

3 Read the passage and fill in the blanks with the key words. (12-4)

Athletic shoes are used for sports. There are _________________ _________________

_________________. Basketball shoes are quite high, while tennis shoes are quite

low. Bowling shoes are _______________ on the bottom and cycling shoes have

special clips. Running shoes are very _______________ and soccer shoes have

cleats on the bottom for digging into _______________. If you _______________

many different sports, you really need many different shoes!

Key Words   many/ play/ grass/ light/ types/ flat/ different

Respond to Questions

Respond to the following questions. (12-5)

Q1 How many pairs of shoes do you own?

A1 I have about ___________________________ pairs of shoes.

Q2 Do you like new shoes or old shoes?

A2 ___________________________ shoes are more comfortable.

Q3 How much does a good pair of shoes cost?

A3 About ___________________________ dollars.

Q4 What kind of shoes are your favorite?

A4 I like ___________________________ .

Q5 What are dress shoes usually made of?

A5 Dress shoes are usually made of ___________________________ .

Q6 What kind of shoes do you wear to the beach?

A6 I wear ___________________________ .

Q7 What type of shoes do you wear in the rain and mud?

A7 We wear ___________________________ .

Q8 Who usually wears boots?

A8 ___________________________ wear boots.

Q9 What kind of shoes are in fashion now?

A9 Right now people wear ___________________________ .

Q10 Do you ever wear slippers?

A10 Yes. I wear slippers ___________________________ .

Personal Experience & Opinion

Read the question and write your own answer. 12-6

Question Talk about your favorite pair of shoes.

Sample Answer

My favorite shoes are my soccer cleats. They are about 2 years old and they're a little bit small. They are black and blue and they are almost worn out. I have played so many soccer games in them. They are good luck to me. Unfortunately, because they're small and worn out, I can't wear them anymore. I need to buy new soccer shoes, but I'm sad about that.

My Answer

- My favorite shoes are ________________________.
- They are ________________________.
- I ________________________ in them.
- They are ________________________ to me.

More Questions

1 If you could have any new shoes, what would they be like?

2 What is more important: comfort or style?

3 What is your favorite place to buy shoes?

Word a little bit   unfortunately

Chapter 13 Post office

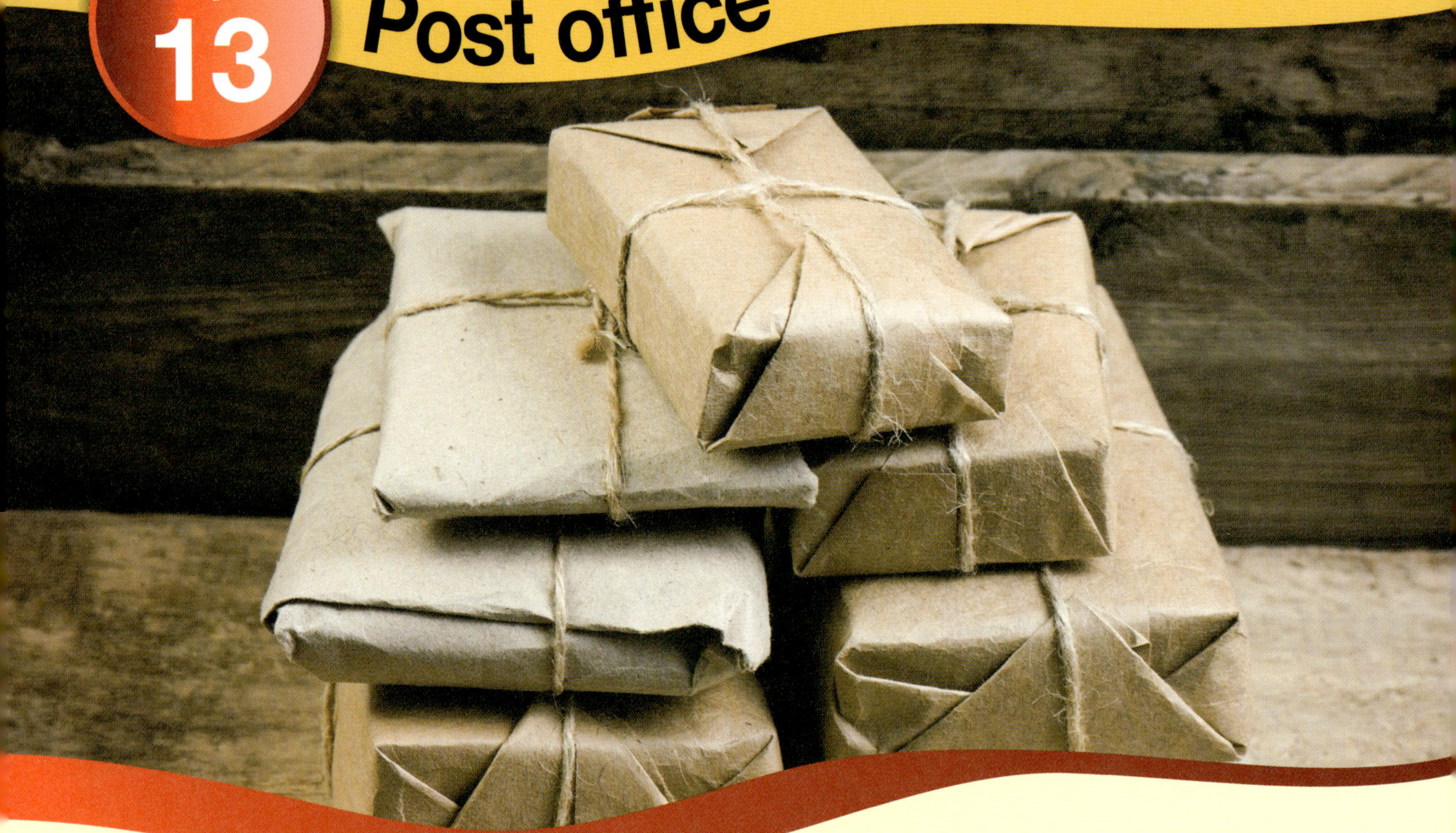

Word Pronunciation

Listen to the following words and repeat them. 13-1

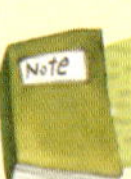

- **package** [pǽkidʒ] *n.* ____________
- **envelope** [énvəlòup] *n.* ____________
- **destination** [dèstənéiʃən] *n.* ____________
- **box** [báks] *n.* ____________
- **postcard** [póustkὰ:*r*d] *n.* ____________
- **deliver** [dilívə*r*] *v.* ____________
- **by air** *ad.* ____________
- **cost** [kɔ:st] *n.* ____________
- **stamp** [stǽmp] *n.* ____________
- **parcel** [pá:*r*sl] *n.* ____________
- **mailbox** [méilbὰks] *n.* ____________
- **address** [ǽdres] *n.* ____________
- **mailman** [méilmæ̀n] *n.* ____________
- **send** [sénd] *v.* ____________
- **by ship** *ad.* ____________

Describe Two Pictures 

Look at the pictures and fill in the blanks with the most suitable words. 13-2

1

A woman is _______________ a man a _______________ .

2

A boy is putting a _______________ on an _______________ .

Situational Conversation

Listen to the conversation and answer the questions. 13-3

Q1 What is the man sending?

Q2 What is the parcel's destination?

Q3 How much will it cost to send?

Read Aloud

1 Read the words aloud. ❙13-4❙

post office	cost	first
depend	far away	heavy
big	fourth	quickly

2 Read the passage aloud. ❙13-4❙

If you need to / send something / to someone, / you need to / go to the post office. / The cost / to send something / depends. / First, / it is more expensive / to send something / far away. / Second, / it is more expensive / to send something heavy. / Third, / it is more expensive / to send something big. / And fourth, / it is more expensive / to send something / quickly.

3 Read the passage and fill in the blanks with the key words. ❙13-4❙

At the post office you can buy stamps ______________ ______________ ______________. A stamp is a little sticker that you put on an envelope that shows that you paid to send it. Stamps usually have little pictures on them. They also have a number on them to ______________ ______________ ______________. We have to put the stamp ______________ the ______________ ______________ of the envelope before putting the letter in a ______________.

Key Words letters/ corner/ in/ to/ the/ upper-right/ mail/ show/ price/ mailbox

Respond to Questions

Respond to the following questions. (13-5)

Q1 How far is the closest post office to your house?

A1 The closest post office is ________________ blocks.

Q2 How often do you go to the post office?

A2 I go about ________________.

Q3 What can you buy at the post office?

A3 I can buy ________________.

Q4 What color are mailboxes in your city?

A4 In my city, mailboxes are ________________.

Q5 How much does it cost to send a letter within your country?

A5 It costs ________________.

Q6 What do you have to write on the envelope?

A6 You have to write ________________.

Q7 What is something you can't send by mail?

A7 You can't send ________________.

Q8 What's the most expensive way to send something?

A8 ________________ is most expensive.

Q9 Do you like to send postcards?

A9 Yes, I ________________.

Q10 What does a mailman do?

A10 He ________________.

Personal Experience & Opinion

Read the question and write your own answer. `13-6`

Question What is the best thing you have received by mail?

Sample Answer

Last year on my birthday I got a package from my uncle. I had to pick it up at the post office. It was a huge heavy box. I took it home and opened it right away. Inside was 50 DVDs! My uncle bought me all of my favorite movies! I was so happy that I called him right away to say thank you. That was the best package I have ever received.

My Answer

- Last ________________, I got ____________ from ________________.
- It was ________________________________.
- Inside was ____________________________.
- I was so ____________ that I ________________.

More Questions

1 Do you know anybody who still sends personal letters?

2 When are the busiest times of year for the post office?

3 If you could make a new stamp, what would be on it?

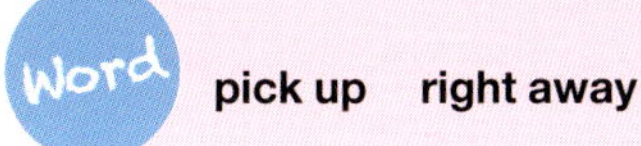
Word **pick up   right away**

Chapter 14

Airport

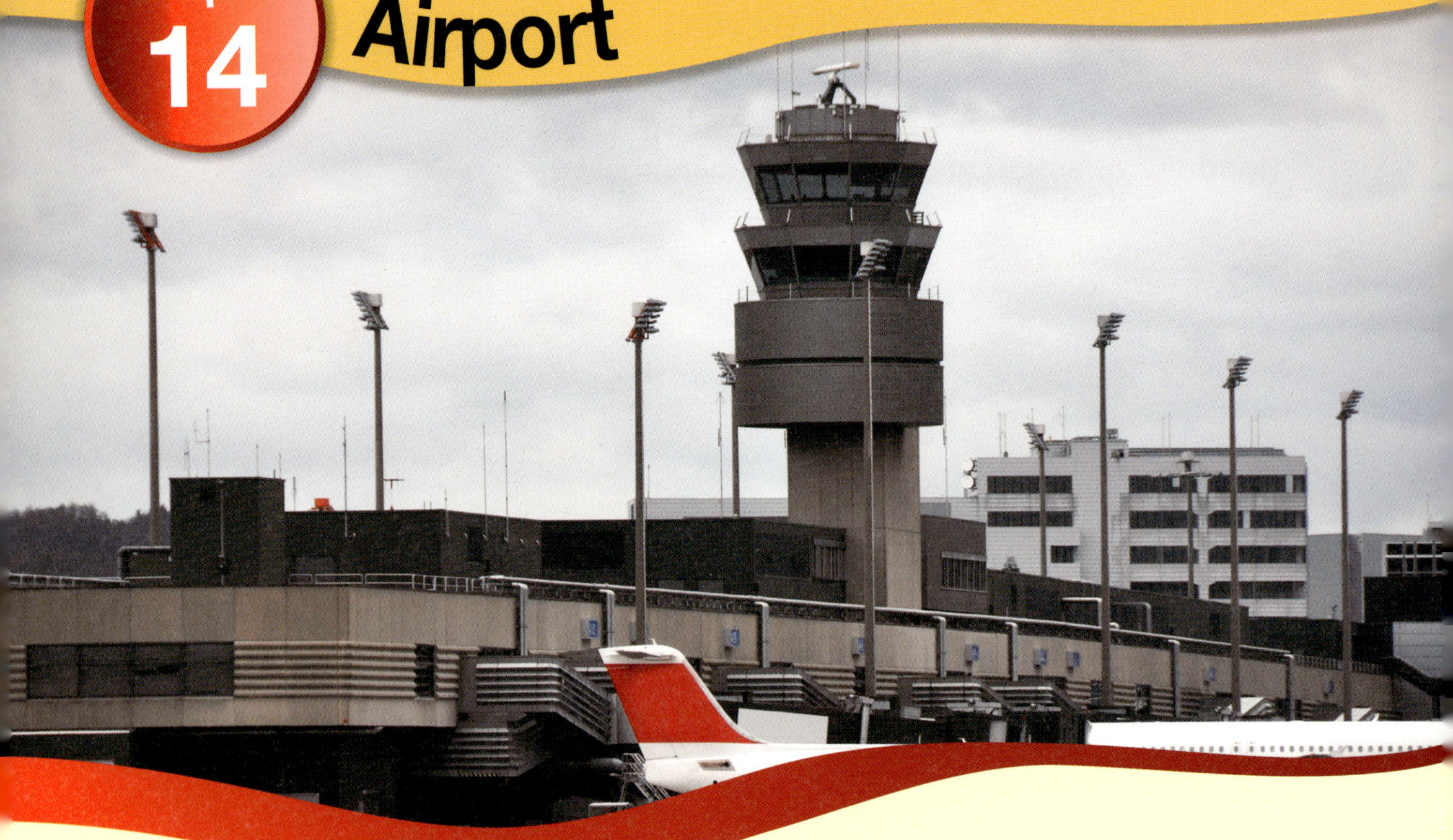

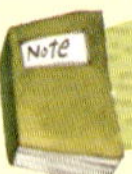

Word Pronunciation

Listen to the following words and repeat them. 14-1

- □ **ticket** [tíkit] *n.* ______________
- □ **terminal** [tə́ːrmənəl] *n.* ______________
- □ **domestic** [dəméstik] *a.* ______________
- □ **gate** [géit] *n.* ______________
- □ **baggage** [bǽgidʒ] *n.* ______________
- □ **customs** [kʌ́stəms] *n.* ______________
- □ **carousel** [kæ̀rəsél] *n.* ______________
- □ **departure** [dipáːrtʃər] *n.* ______________
- □ **flight** [fláit] *n.* ______________
- □ **international** [ìntərnǽʃənəl] *a.* ______________
- □ **security** [sikjúːərəti] *n.* ______________
- □ **beep** [bíːp] *v.* ______________
- □ **passport** [pǽspɔːrt] *n.* ______________
- □ **immigration** [ìməgréiʃən] *n.* ______________
- □ **arrival** [əráivəl] *n.* ______________

Look at the pictures and fill in the blanks with the most suitable words. (14-2)

1

A woman is putting her ______________ through the x-ray ______________.

2

A man is giving his ticket to a ______________ ______________.

Situational Conversation

Listen to the conversation and answer the questions. (14-3)

Q1 Where is the man going?

Q2 When does the next flight leave?

Q3 How much is a first-class seat?

Read Aloud

1 **Read the words aloud.** (14-4)

more than	section	international terminal
other countries	domestic terminal	different parts
totally different	right terminal	won't be able to

2 **Read the passage aloud.** (14-4)

Large airports / usually have / more than one terminal, / or / section of the airport. / There is usually / an international terminal / for planes / going to other countries. / For planes / travelling in the same country, / there is / a domestic terminal. / Sometimes / the terminals are / different parts / of the same building. / But sometimes / the terminals are / totally different buildings. / You have to go / to the right terminal / or you won't be able to find / your flight!

3 **Read the passage and fill in the blanks with the key words.** (14-4)

Before you get on a plane you have to _______________ _______________ security. You have to _______________ _______________ _______________ and then put your bag through the x-ray machine. Then you have to walk through a security gate. The security gate will beep if you have any metal. The security guards will check to make sure you don't have anything bad. They might also open your bag and _______________ _______________ . Hopefully they don't make a big mess!

Key Words   wait/ though/ go/ inside/ in/ look/ in

Respond to Questions

Respond to the following questions. (14-5)

Q1 Do you have a passport?

A1 ______________________________ .

Q2 How many flights have you taken?

A2 I've taken about ______________________________ flights.

Q3 How often do you go to the airport to pick someone up?

A3 Probably ______________________________ .

Q4 What do you call the places where the passengers leave to get on their flight?

A4 They are called ______________________________ .

Q5 What do you have to show at Customs and Immigration?

A5 I have to show my ______________________________ .

Q6 How many bags do you usually take when you travel?

A6 I usually take ______________________________ .

Q7 What can you see on the Arrivals and Departures board?

A7 I can see ______________________________ .

Q8 What is your favorite airline?

A8 I like ______________________________ .

Q9 What are you not allowed to take through security?

A9 ______________________________ .

Q10 What do you do at the baggage carousel?

A10 I wait for ______________________________ to come out.

Personal Experience & Opinion

Read the question and write your own answer. (14-6)

Question   What is the longest you have waited in an airport?

Sample Answer

One time I went to the airport with my parents to pick up my uncle. His flight was late. The arrivals board said it was 2 hours late, but actually it was 4 hours late. We couldn't go anywhere and just had to wait in the airport. We went into every store and walked through the whole airport many times. Even though it was a long time, I wasn't bored. It was interesting to see all the people.

My Answer

- One time I ________________________________ .
- The arrivals[departures] board said it was ________________ .
- I had to wait ________________________ .
- It was ________________ to ________________ .

More Questions

1 What services does the airport in your city have?

2 What is the busiest airport you have been to?

3 What are the different ways you can get from the airport to downtown?

Chapter 15 Airplane

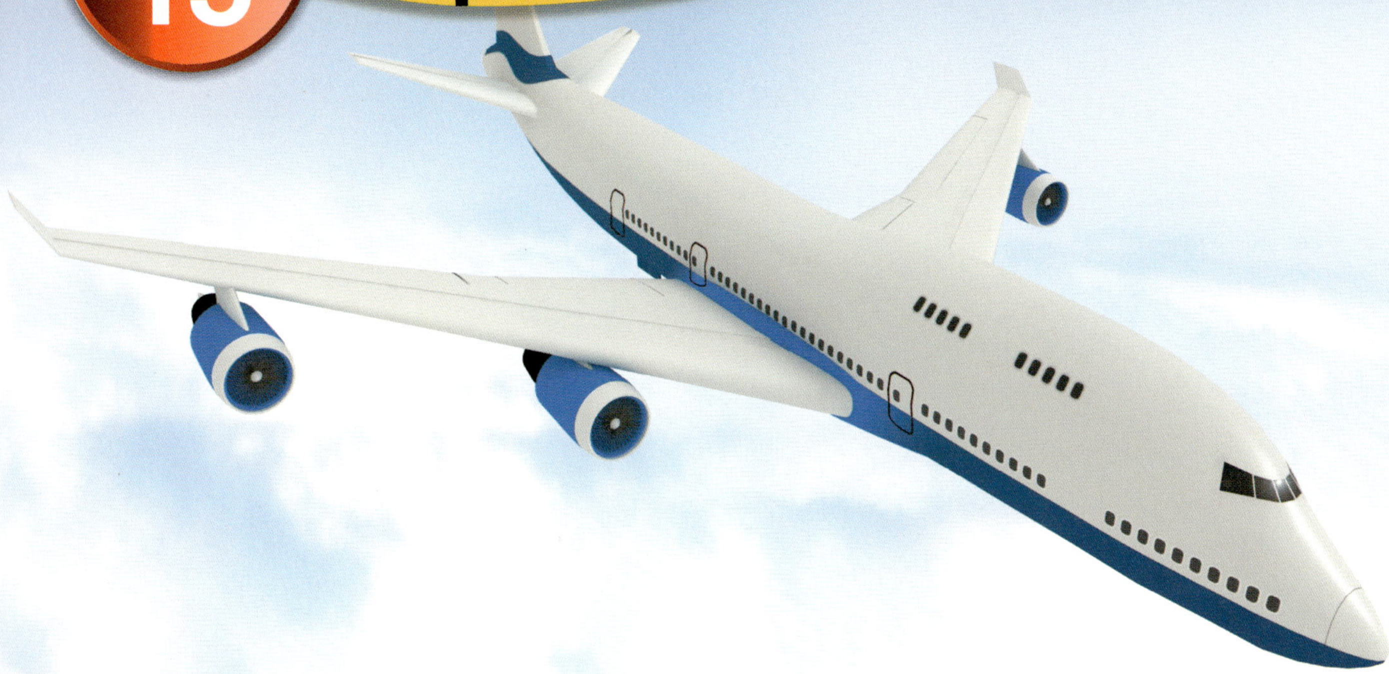

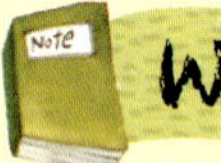

Word Pronunciation

Listen to the following words and repeat them. 15-1

- □ **compartment** [kəmpáːrtmənt] *n.* ________
- □ **tray** [tréi] *n.* ________
- □ **attendant** [əténdənt] *n.* ________
- □ **cabin** [kǽbin] *n.* ________
- □ **passenger** [pǽsəndʒər] *n.* ________
- □ **aisle** [áil] *n.* ________
- □ **take off** *v.* ________
- □ **turbulence** [tə́ːrbjələns] *n.* ________
- □ **headphones** [hédfòuns] *n.* ________
- □ **arrive** [əráiv] *v.* ________
- □ **cockpit** [kákpit] *n.* ________
- □ **first-class** *n.* ________
- □ **cart** [káːrt] *n.* ________
- □ **window** [wíndou] *n.* ________
- □ **land** [lǽnd] *v.* ________

Describe Two Pictures 

Look at the pictures and fill in the blanks with the most suitable words. 15-2

1

A man is putting his ______________ in the overhead ______________.

2

A girl is wearing ______________ and ______________ a movie.

Situational Conversation

Listen to the conversation and answer the questions. (15-3)

Q1 What will the passenger drink?

Q2 When will the plane arrive?

Q3 What does the attendant offer the passenger to eat?

Read Aloud

1 **Read the words aloud.** (15-4)

at the front of	cockpit	full of
instruments	cabin	passengers
a first-class section	comfortable but expensive	most people

2 **Read the passage aloud.** (15-4)

At the front of an airplane / is the cockpit. / This is / where the pilot and the co-pilot sit. / The cockpit / is full of / instruments and computers. / Behind the cockpit / is the cabin, / where passengers sit. / There is / a first-class section, / which is very comfortable / but expensive. / There is also / a large economy class section, / where most people sit.

3 **Read the passage and fill in the blanks with the key words.** (15-4)

Being a flight attendant can be a ______________ job. You have to push a cart down ______________ ______________ ______________ and give food and drinks to passengers. If anyone has a problem, you have to ______________ it. You need to be ______________ even if everybody else is very excited, angry, or worried. The good thing about the job is that you get to travel to ______________ ______________ !

Key Words   many/ difficult/ calm/ places/ solve/ different/ a/ aisle/ small

Respond to Questions

Respond to the following questions. (15-5)

Q1 How many times have you been on a plane?
A1 I have been on a plane _______________ times.

Q2 Do you like a window or an aisle seat?
A2 I prefer _______________ .

Q3 What do you have to do before taking off and landing?
A3 I have to _______________ .

Q4 Where did you go on your first flight?
A4 I went to _______________ .

Q5 Do you know anyone who is scared of flying?
A5 _______________ is scared of flying.

Q6 What do you usually do during a flight?
A6 I like to sleep or _______________ .

Q7 Do you get scared when there is turbulence?
A7 I _______________ .

Q8 What do the buttons above the seat do?
A8 Turn on the light and _______________ .

Q9 What do you think of airplane bathrooms?
A9 They're _______________ .

Q10 What quality does a flight attendant need to have?
A10 They need to be _______________ .

Personal Experience & Opinion

Read the question and write your own answer. (15-6)

Question What was the longest flight you've taken?

Sample Answer

The longest flight I have taken was from Los Angeles to Hong Kong. It was over 14 hours! I watched four movies and had a long sleep. We ate several meals on the flight. It was difficult to sit in my seat for that long. I had to take breaks and walk up and down the aisle. Everybody was very happy when we finally landed.

My Answer

- The longest flight I have taken was ________________________________.
- It was over ________________________________.
- I had to ________________________________.
- Everybody was ________________ when we finally landed.

More Questions

1 What do you dislike about being on an airplane?

2 Would you like to be a flight attendant? Why or why not?

3 Have you ever seen inside the cockpit?

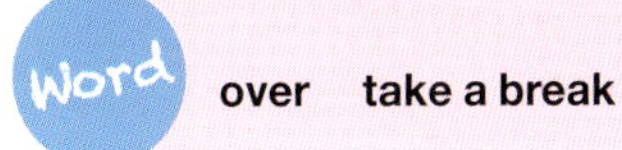

Word over   take a break

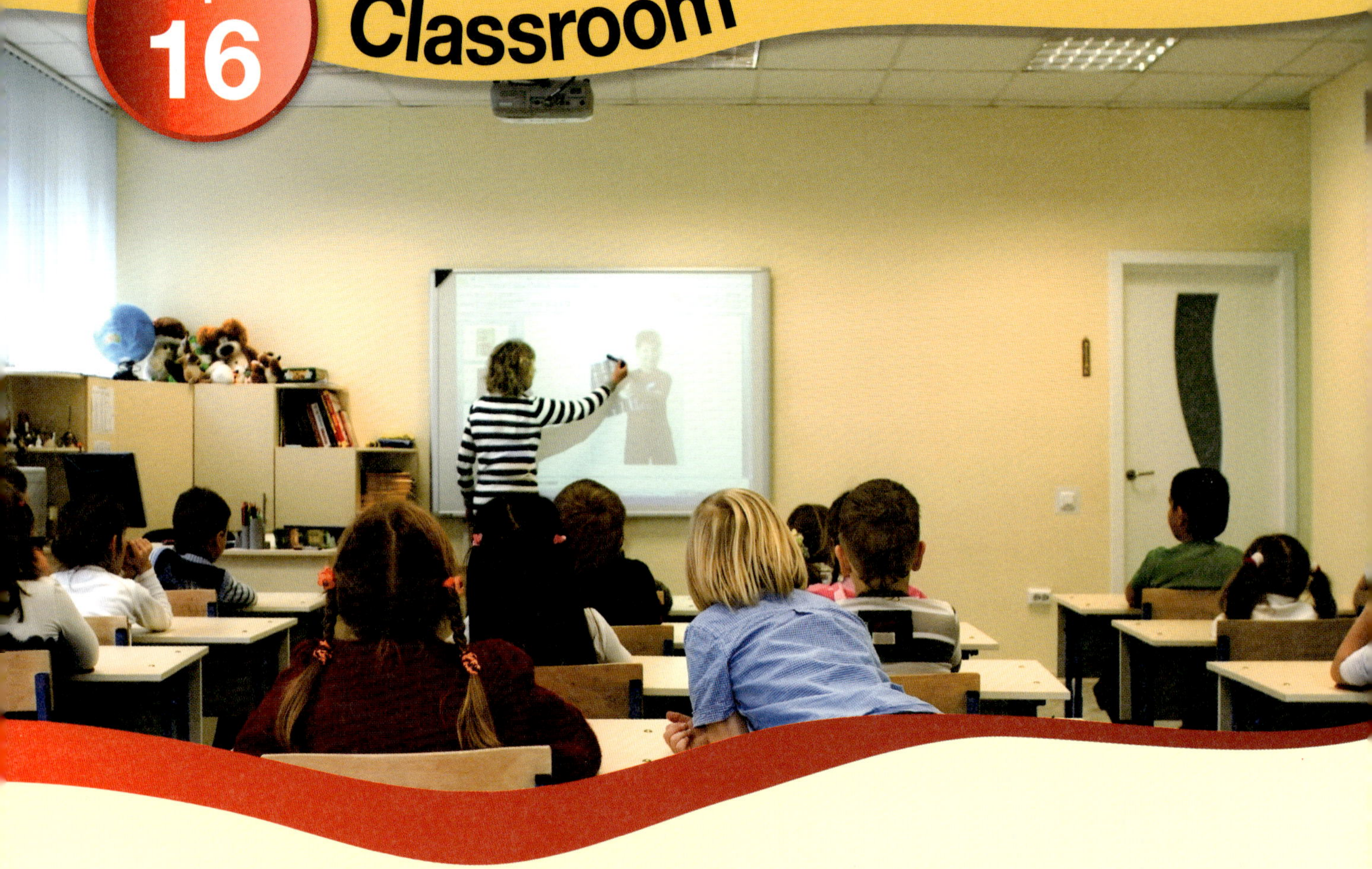

Word Pronunciation

Listen to the following words and repeat them. 16-1

- **textbook** [tékstbùk] *n.* _______________
- **desk** [désk] *n.* _______________
- **face** [féis] *v.* _______________
- **punish** [pʌ́niʃ] *v.* _______________
- **subject** [sʌ́bdʒikt] *n.* _______________
- **poster** [póustər] *n.* _______________
- **homework** [hóumwə̀rk] *n.* _______________
- **arrange** [əréindʒ] *v.* _______________

- **blackboard** [blǽkbɔ̀rd] *n.* _______________
- **row** [róu] *n.* _______________
- **behave** [bihéiv] *v.* _______________
- **seat** [síːt] *n.* _______________
- **uniform** [júːnəfɔ̀rm] *n.* _______________
- **comfortable** [kʌ́mfərtəbl] *a.* _______________
- **bookshelf** [búkʃèlf] *n.* _______________

Describe Two Pictures 

Look at the pictures and fill in the blanks with the most suitable words. ❚16-2❚

1

A teacher is writing on the ______________ at the front of ____________.

2

A student is ____________ his ____________ to ask a question.

Situational Conversation

Listen to the conversation and answer the questions. 16-3

Q1 What page should students turn to in their book?

Q2 What does the student want to do?

Q3 How many times has the student left class?

Read Aloud

1 **Read the words aloud.** 16-4

there are	arrange	in rows
facing	arranged	in a circle
sit together	in groups	could be

2 **Read the passage aloud.** 16-4

There are / different ways / to arrange a classroom. / Many classrooms / have student desks / in rows, / all facing/to the front. / Other classrooms / have desks / arranged in a circle. / Some classrooms / have large tables / where students sit together / in groups. / The teacher's desk / could be at the front, / the back, / or the side of the classroom. / These different ways / are good / for different kinds of learning.

3 **Read the passage and fill in the blanks with the key words.** 16-4

A teacher has to do many things. Sometimes she stands at the front of the class and ______________ ______________ all the students. She might ______________ ______________ the ______________ to help students learn. Sometimes she has to walk around and ______________ ______________ ______________ . She has to make sure students ______________ ______________ and do all of their work. Sometimes this means she has to ______________ students.

Key Words   well/ behave/ talks/ punish/ blackboard/ on/ write/ separately/ students/ to/ help

Respond to Questions

Respond to the following questions. (16-5)

Q1 How much time do you spend each day in a classroom?
A1 I spend about _________________________ hours.

Q2 Do you like sitting in a classroom?
A2 I _________________________.

Q3 Can you choose your seat in your classroom?
A3 No, our teacher tells us _________________________.

Q4 How many students are there in your class?
A4 There are _________________________ students.

Q5 What is your favorite school subject?
A5 I really like _________________________.

Q6 Do you like to have a male or female teacher?
A6 I like to have a _________________________ teacher.

Q7 What can you not do in your classroom?
A7 I can't _________________________ in my classroom.

Q8 Do you have to wear a uniform to class?
A8 _________________________.

Q9 What happens if you are late for class?
A9 I have to _________________________.

Q10 Is your classroom comfortable?
A10 _________________________.

Personal Experience & Opinion

Read the question and write your own answer. (16-6)

Question What does your classroom look like?

Sample Answer

Our classroom is nice. It has windows on one side and beautiful travel posters on the other side. Below the posters is a bench where we put our stuff. The teacher sits at the back and all the students face the blackboard. On the back wall is a big bookshelf with many interesting books. My classroom is usually quite cool, even in summer. I like that.

My Answer

- Our classroom is ___________________________.
- It has ___________________________.
- On the back wall is ___________________________.
- My classroom is usually ___________________________.

More Questions

1 Do you think uniforms are a good idea?

2 Are you happy with where you sit in class?

3 What would you change about your classroom?

Word quite   even

Chapter 17

Zoo

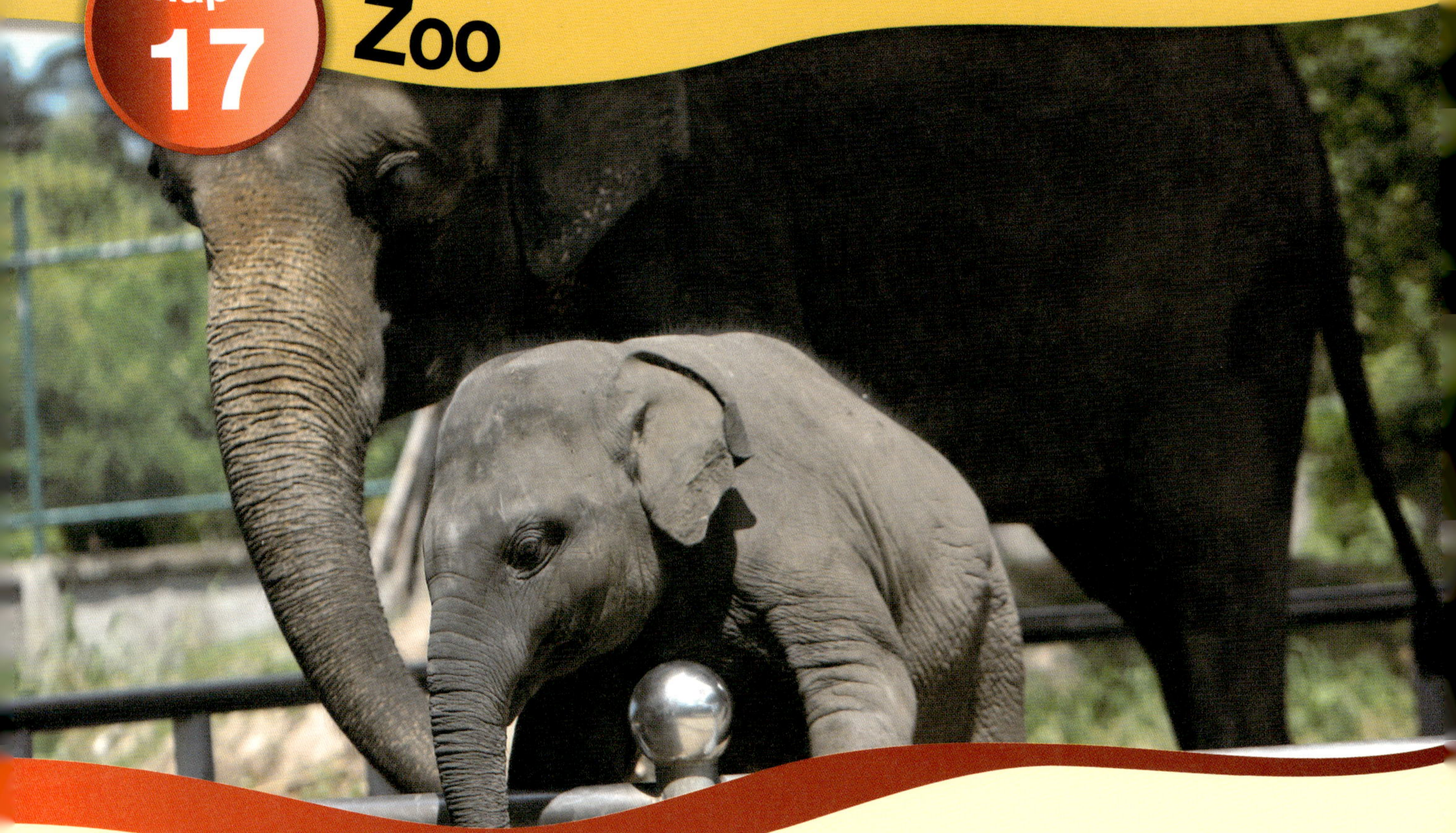

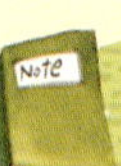

Word Pronunciation

Listen to the following words and repeat them. 17-1

- **touch** [tʌ́tʃ] *v.* ______________
- **education** [èdʒukéiʃən] *n.* ______________
- **cage** [kéidʒ] *n.* ______________
- **exotic** [igzɑ́tik] *a.* ______________
- **aquarium** [əkwέːəriəm] *n.* ______________
- **trainer** [tréinər] *n.* ______________
- **stinky** [stíŋki] *a.* ______________
- **petting zoo** *n.* ______________
- **pen** [pén] *n.* ______________
- **wild** [wáild] *a.* ______________
- **creature** [kríːtʃər] *n.* ______________
- **reptile** [réptail] *n.* ______________
- **feed** [fíːd] *v.* ______________
- **pet** [pét] *n.* ______________
- **space** [spéis] *n.* ______________

Describe Two Pictures 

Look at the pictures and fill in the blanks with the most suitable words. ▌17-2▐

1

A trainer is giving some ______________ to a ______________ .

2

Several ______________ are watching a ______________ .

Situational Conversation

Listen to the conversation and answer the questions. 17-3

Q1 Where are the lions located?

Q2 When is feeding time?

Q3 What do the lions eat?

Read Aloud

1 **Read the words aloud.** (17-4)

pay	are kept	in cages or pens
wander	should be	in the wild
zoo	especially	for education

2 **Read the passage aloud.** (17-4)

A zoo / is a place / where we can pay / to see animals. / The animals / are kept / in cages or pens / where they can play / and wander. / Some people think that / zoos are not good places / for animals. / They think that / animals should be left / to live in the wild. / But zoos help people, / especially children, / learn about animals. / They are a place / for education.

3 **Read the passage and fill in the blanks with the key words.** (17-4)

At my local zoo, there are many _____________. You can see crocodiles and alligators that like to live in _____________. You can also see snakes and iguanas in large glass _____________. There are also _____________ that move very slowly. The place for reptiles is very hot because these animals _____________ live in hot places. It is fun to see _____________ like these at the zoo.

Key Words giant/ creatures/ swamps/ reptiles/ turtles/ usually/ exotic/ cages

Respond to Questions

Respond to the following questions. 17-5

Q1 How often do you visit a zoo?

A1　Probably ________________________________.

Q2 Have you ever been to an aquarium?

A2　________________________________.

Q3 What is your favorite animal?

A3　I really like ________________________________.

Q4 Do you think it is OK to keep animals in zoos?

A4　________________________________.

Q5 Is it OK to feed the animals in a zoo?

A5　________________________________.

Q6 What is the most amazing animal you have seen?

A6　I think ________________________ is the most amazing animal.

Q7 If you could have any animal as a pet, what would you have?

A7　I would like ________________________________.

Q8 Would you like to work in a zoo?

A8　________________________________.

Q9 Have you been to a petting zoo, where you can touch the animals?

A9　________________________________.

Q10 What is the cutest kind of baby animal?

A10　The cutest are ________________________________.

Personal Experience & Opinion

Read the question and write your own answer. 〔17-6〕

Question When was the first time you went to a zoo?

Sample Answer

The first time I went to a zoo was when I was five years old. I went with my father. He bought some ice cream for me and we walked around to see all the animals. I was very excited. My favorite part was watching the penguins jump into the water. The zoo was very big and we walked everywhere, so I was very tired. I fell asleep in the car on the way home.

My Answer

- The first time I went to a zoo was when ________________________ .
- I went with ____ .
- My favorite part was ______________________________ .
- The zoo was ____________ , so I ____________________ .

More Questions

1 What should you NOT do in a zoo?

2 What animal are you most afraid of?

3 Which animal do you think needs the most space in a zoo?

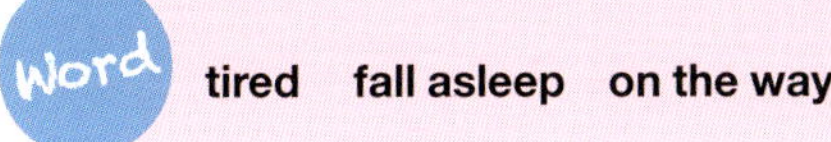

Word tired   fall asleep   on the way

Chapter 18

Wedding

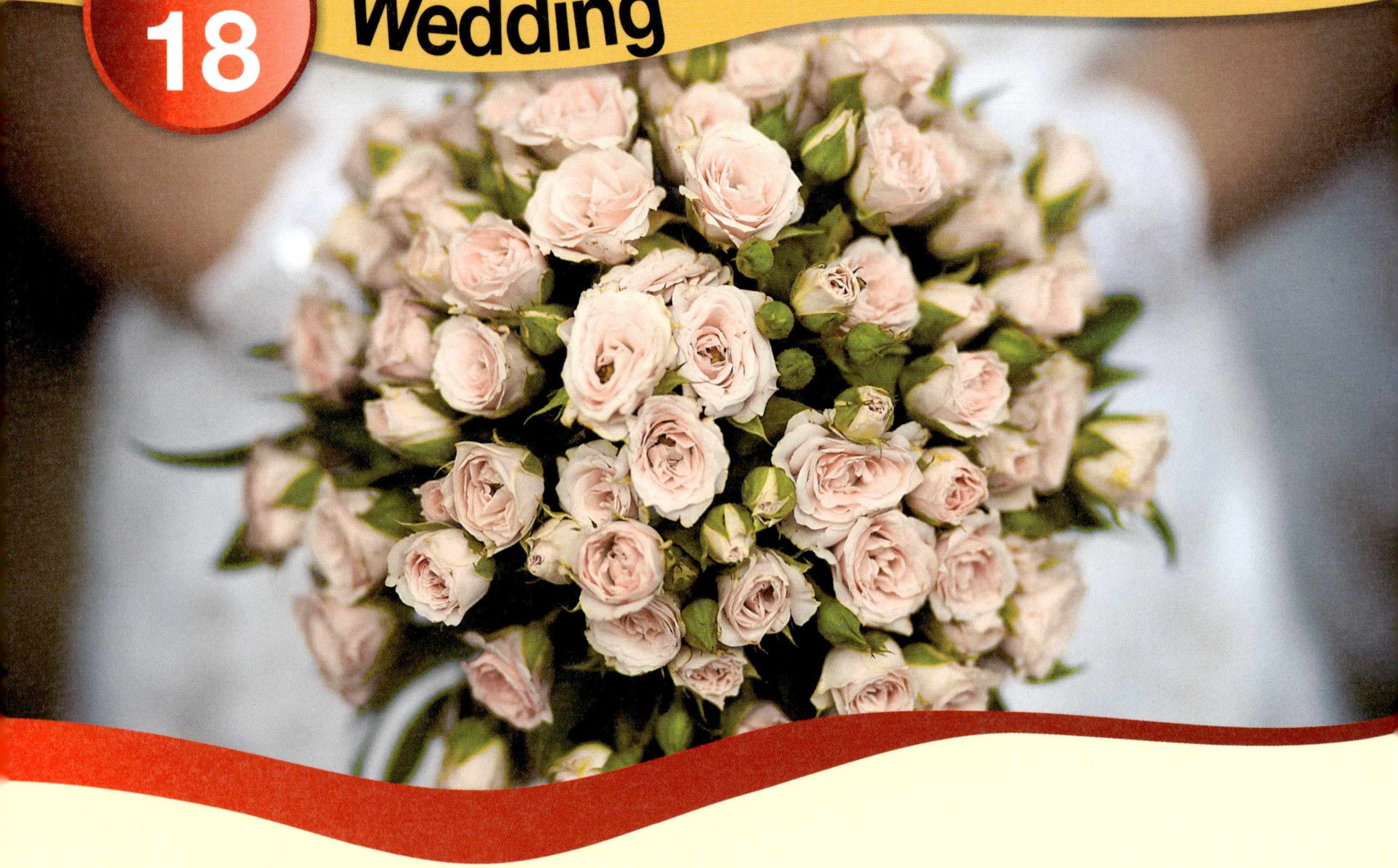

Word Pronunciation

Listen to the following words and repeat them. ❙18-1❙

□ **bride** [bráid] *n.* ____________

□ **formal** [fɔ́:rməl] *a.* ____________

□ **enter** [éntər] *v.* ____________

□ **reception** [risépʃən] *n.* ____________

□ **happen** [hǽpən] *v.* ____________

□ **choose** [tʃú:z] *v.* ____________

□ **appearance** [əpí:ərəns] *n.* ____________

□ **international** [ìntərnǽʃənəl] *a.* ____________

□ **groom** [grú:m] *n.* ____________

□ **clothes** [klóuðz] *n.* ____________

□ **wedding hall** *n.* ____________

□ **attend** [əténd] *v.* ____________

□ **get married** *ph.* ____________

□ **usual** [jú:ʒuəl] *a.* ____________

□ **marry** [mǽri] *v.* ____________

□ **take place** *ph.* ____________

Describe Two Pictures 

Look at the pictures and fill in the blanks with the most suitable words. (18-2)

1

A bride and ______________ are standing at the front of the

______________ .

2

People in formal clothes are ______________ a ______________ hall.

Situational Conversation

Listen to the conversation and answer the questions. 18-3

Q1 What time is the reception?

Q2 Where will the reception take place?

Q3 How many people will attend?

Read Aloud

1 **Read the words aloud.** ◀18-4▶

happen	get married	choose
a wedding hall	usual	anywhere
on the beach	on a boat	on top of

2 **Read the passage aloud.** ◀18-4▶

Weddings can happen / in different places. / Some people / get married / in a church. / Other people / choose to get married / in a wedding hall. / Those are / the usual places, / but it's possible / to get married / anywhere. / Some couples / have a wedding / on the beach, / or on a boat, / or on the top of a mountain. / I would like to get married / in a movie theater.

3 **Read the passage and fill in the blanks with the key words.** ◀18-4▶

Many of the people at a wedding have _______________ _______________.
The man who is getting _______________ is called the _______________. He usually has a person with him call the "best man." The best man is usually the with groom's _______________ or friend. The woman who is getting married is called the _______________. She also has someone with her, called the "maid of honor." This is usually her _______________ or friend.

Key Words names/ bride/ sister/ brother/ groom/ special/ married

Respond to Questions 

Respond to the following questions. (18-5)

Q1 What do you think is a good age to get married?

A1   I think ________________________________ is a good age.

Q2 Where do you want to get married?

A2   I want to get married in ________________________________ .

Q3 How many weddings have you attended?

A3   I've attended ________________________________ weddings.

Q4 How old were your parents when they got married?

A4   My father was ________________ and my mother was ________________ .

Q5 Where is a good place for a honeymoon?

A5   I think ________________________________ is a good place for a honeymoon.

Q6 What is the best season to get married?

A6   I think ________________________________ is best.

Q7 Would you marry someone 10 years older than you?

A7   ________________________________ .

Q8 How important is appearance in choosing a person to marry?

A8   I think it's ________________________________ .

Q9 How many children would you like to have?

A9   I want ________________________________ .

Q10 Do you think international marriages are okay?

A10   ________________________________ .

Personal Experience & Opinion 

Read the question and write your own answer. (18-6)

Question   What kind of personality should a good husband or a good wife have?

Sample Answer

I think a good husband or wife should be kind. Without kindness, there might be problems in the family. I also think they should be honest. We must tell the truth at all times to the person we are married to. I think that good husbands and wives are not selfish. They think about the other person or the children before they think of themselves.

My Answer

- I think a good husband or wife should be ________________________ .
- I also think they should be ________________________ .
- We must ________________________ to the person we are married to.
- I think that good husbands and wives are not ________________________ .

More Questions

1 Would you ever accept an arranged marriage?

2 In your country, what are traditional wedding clothes?

3 What type of person do you think your parents want you to marry?

Word   kindness   at all times   selfish

Funeral

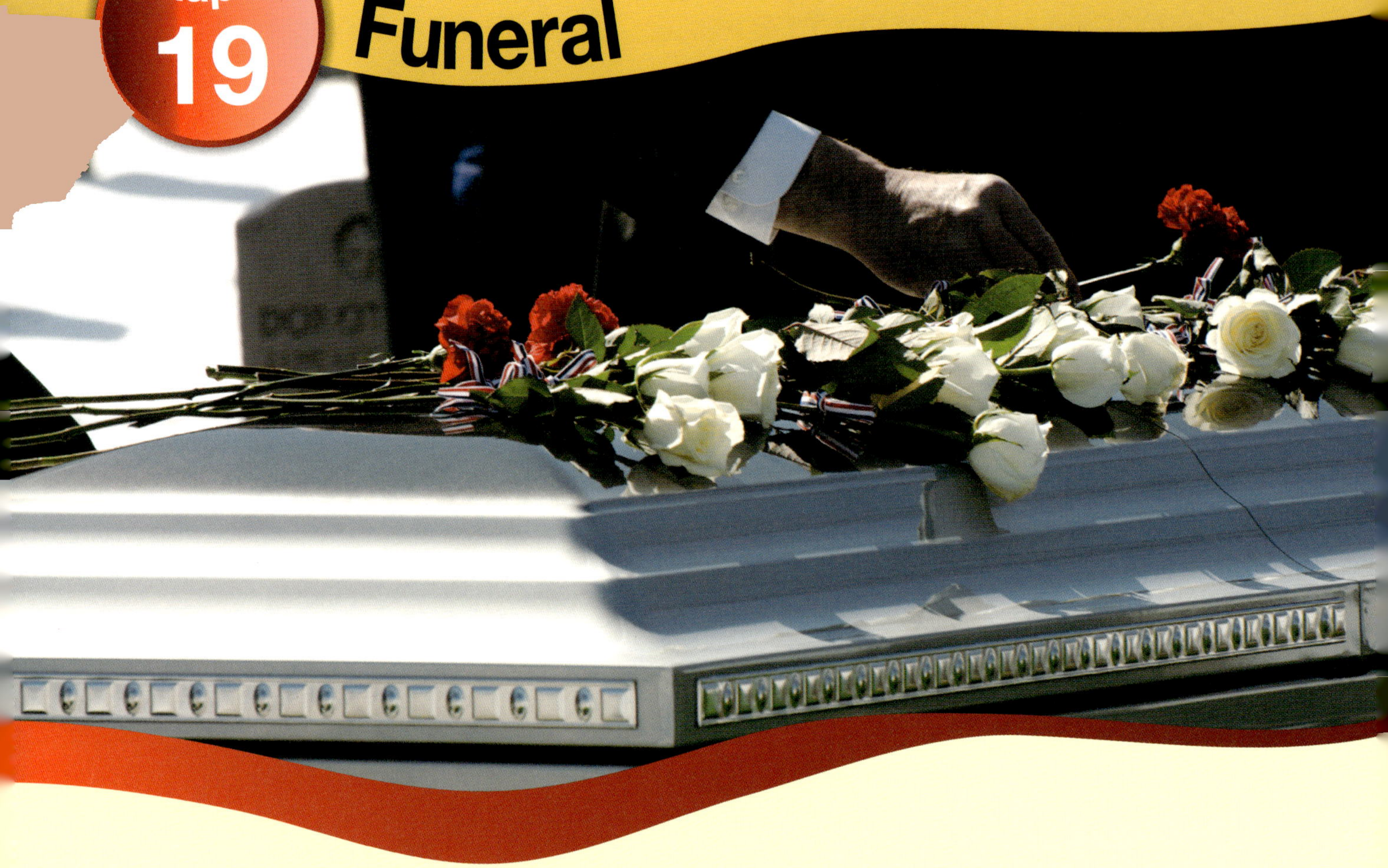

 Word Pronunciation

Listen to the following words and repeat them. ◖19-1◗

- **cry** [krái] *v.* _______________
- **dirt** [dɔ́:rt] *n.* _______________
- **hearse** [hɔ́:rs] *n.* _______________
- **dead** [déd] *a.* _______________
- **cemetery** [sémitèri] *n.* _______________
- **pass away** *v.* _______________
- **cremate** [krí:meit] *v.* _______________
- **memory** [méməri] *n.* _______________

- **grave** [gréiv] *n.* _______________
- **respectful** [rispéktfəl] *a.* _______________
- **coffin** [kɔ́:fin] *n.* _______________
- **procession** [prəséʃən] *n.* _______________
- **eulogy** [júːlədʒi] *n.* _______________
- **attend** [əténd] *v.* _______________
- **bury** [béri] *v.* _______________

Look at the pictures and fill in the blanks with the most suitable words. 19-2

Several people dressed in _____________ are crying.

A man is putting ____________ on a ____________.

Situational Conversation

Listen to the conversation and answer the questions. 〔19-3〕

Q1 What is the dead man's name?

Q2 What is the speaker's relationship to the dead man?

Q3 Where will he be buried?

Read Aloud

1 Read the words aloud. (❙19-4❙)

a special kind of	funeral	hearse
carry	coffin	the dead person
behind	should be	respectful

2 Read the passage aloud. (❙19-4❙)

In many countries, / there is / a special kind of car / used for funerals. / It is called / a hearse. / The hearse / is long and black / and it carries the coffin / with the dead person / to the funeral. / Often / the hearse / drives very slowly / with the other cars / behind it. / When / people see a hearse, / they know / they should be / quiet and respectful.

3 Read the passage and fill in the blanks with the key words. (❙19-4❙)

There is often special music at a ______________. In some countries, there is certain music that people always ______________. In some countries, ______________ follow the funeral procession through the streets. Sometimes the music is something that the ______________ person really liked. At some funerals, people play the guitar or piano. To me, the music is always the ______________ part.

Key Words saddest/ dead/ musicians/ funeral/ play

Respond to Questions

Respond to the following questions. (19-5)

Q1 How many times have you been to a funeral?

A1 I have ________________________.

Q2 What color of clothes do people wear to a funeral in your country?

A2 People usually wear ________________________.

Q3 How old do you want to live until?

A3 I want to live until I am ________________________.

Q4 What do you give as a gift when someone dies?

A4 Usually we give ________________________.

Q5 Do you think cemeteries are scary?

A5 ________________________.

Q6 Who do you want to give your eulogy?

A6 I want ________________________ to give my eulogy.

Q7 Are you afraid of dying?

A7 ________________________.

Q8 Has someone close to you died?

A8 Yes, ________________________ died.

Q9 Do you know another way to say that someone died?

A9 ________________________.

Q10 Who will miss you the most when you're gone?

A10 I think ________________________ will.

Personal Experience & Opinion

Read the question and write your own answer. `19-6`

Question Who do you want to attend your funeral?

Sample Answer

I want just a small funeral. The most important people are my family. I want my whole family at my funeral. Then there are my friends. I have about 10 close friends that I want to come. They can bring their families too. Then I have uncles, aunts, and cousins. They should also be there. I guess that's not so small.

My Answer

- I want a ________________________ funeral.
- The most important people are ________________________ .
- I have about ____________ that I want to come.
- Then I have ________________________ .

More Questions

1 What kind of music do you want at your funeral?

2 Do you want to be buried or cremated?

3 Do you have a sad funeral story?

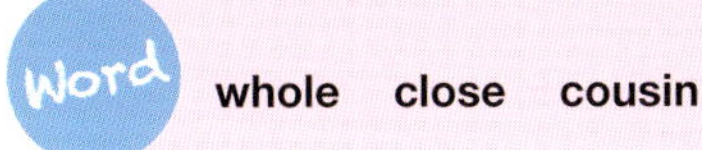

Word whole   close   cousin

Party

Word Pronunciation

Listen to the following words and repeat them. (20-1)

- **talk** [tɔ́ːk] *v.* _______________
- **fun** [fʌ́n] *n.* _______________
- **Christmas** [krísməs] *n.* _______________
- **food** [fúːd] *n.* _______________
- **surprise** [sərpráiz] *n.* _______________
- **restaurant** [réstərənt] *n.* _______________
- **present** [prézənt] *n.* _______________
- **game** [géim] *n.* _______________

- **laugh** [lǽf] *v.* _______________
- **graduation** [græ̀dʒəwéiʃən] *n.* _______________
- **prepare** [pripέər] *v.* _______________
- **New Year's Eve** *n.* _______________
- **birthday** [bə́ːrθdèi] *n.* _______________
- **cake** [kéik] *n.* _______________
- **amusement park** *n.* _______________

Describe Two Pictures 

Look at the pictures and fill in the blanks with the most suitable words. (20-2)

1

Several people are talking and ___________ in a ___________ .

2

A boy is ___________ out candles on a birthday ___________ .

Listen to the conversation and answer the questions. ❨20-3❩

Q1 Where will the birthday party be?

Q2 What should the woman bring?

Q3 How old will Joe be?

Read Aloud

1 Read the words aloud. (20-4)

reason	have a party	birthday
common	on big holidays	New Year
celebrate	graduation	for the fun of

2 Read the passage aloud. (20-4)

There are / so many different reasons / to have a party. / Birthdays / are / one common time, / but we also have parties / on big holidays / like New Year and Christmas. / You can have a party / to celebrate something / like graduation, / getting a new job, / or having a child. / Or, / you can just have a party / for the fun of it.

3 Read the passage and fill in the blanks with the key words. (20-4)

My favorite _____________ of a good party is food. Different parties have _____________ _____________ of food, but I love it all. Many people spend a long time _____________ food for a party. I think it's good to _____________ them that they did a good job. We can do this by eating a lot. My friends _____________ say I like food more than I like them. It's _____________ true, but not quite.

Key Words sometimes/ almost/ part/ kinds/ show/ different/ preparing

Respond to Questions

Respond to the following questions. (20-5)

Q1 How often do you go to parties?

A1 I go about ______________________________ .

Q2 What is your favorite kind of party?

A2 I really like ______________________________ parties.

Q3 What kind of cake do you like on your birthday?

A3 I like ______________________________ the best.

Q4 Have you ever been to a surprise party?

A4 Yes, for ______________________________ .

Q5 Where is the best place to have a party?

A5 I like having a party in ______________________________ .

Q6 What is a good reason NOT to go to a party?

A6 ______________________________ .

Q7 Do you like to talk to a lot of people at parties?

A7 ______________________________ .

Q8 Do you know anyone who goes to too many parties?

A8 ______________________________ goes to parties every week!

Q9 Does your family have parties?

A9 ______________________________ .

Q10 Is there anything bad about a party?

A10 ______________________________ .

Personal Experience & Opinion 

Read the question and write your own answer. ❚20-6❚

Question   What was the best party you have ever had?

Sample Answer

The best party I've ever had was my birthday party last year. My parents took me and all of my friends to the amusement park. We went on rides all afternoon. Then we went out for pizza and cake. Finally, my friends gave me lots of presents. I got a lot of nice things, and even a new computer from my parents.

My Answer

- The best party I've ever had was ____________________________ .
- We had the party at ____________________________ .
- We had[ate] ____________________________ .
- Finally, ____________________________ .

More Questions

1   What kind of games to you like to play at parties?

2   If you could have a party anywhere, where would you have it?

3   Do you prefer big parties or small parties?

Word   ride   prefer

Computers

Word Pronunciation

Listen to the following words and repeat them. `21-1`

- **laptop** [lǽptàp] *n.* ___________
- **broken** [bróukən] *a.* ___________
- **information** [ìnfərméiʃən] *n.* ________
- **tower** [táuər] *n.* ___________
- **mouse** [máus] *n.* ___________
- **webcam** [wébkæm] *n.* ___________
- **website** [websait] *n.* ___________
- **online** [ənláin] *ad.* ___________

- **keyboard** [kíːbɔ̀ːrd] *n.* ___________
- **chatting** [tʃǽtiŋ] *n.* ___________
- **generation** [dʒènəréiʃən] *n.* _______
- **monitor** [mánitər] *n.* ___________
- **printer** [príntər] *n.* ___________
- **desktop** [désktàp] *n.* ___________
- **email** [ìːmeil] *n.* ___________

Look at the pictures and fill in the blanks with the most suitable words. 21-2

1

A man is working on a ____________ on the ____________.

2

A young ____________ is using a computer in a ____________.

Situational Conversation

Listen to the conversation and answer the questions. (21-3)

Q1 What does the man want to buy?

Q2 How much can the man spend?

Q3 What color does the man want?

Read Aloud

1 **Read the words aloud.** (21-4)

very good	grown up	at home
including	chatting	listening to music
naturally	different from	not totally comfortable with

2 **Read the passage aloud.** (21-4)

Young people are / very good / with computers. / Most children / have grown up / with a computer / at home / and computers / in school. / They can use computers / for everything, / including playing games, / studying, / chatting, / finding information, / listening to music / and watching movies. / We use computers / naturally / as a part of life. / This is / different / from the older generations. / Some of them / are still not totally comfortable / with computers.

3 **Read the passage and fill in the blanks with the key words.** (21-4)

A computer has many important _____________. Firstly, there is the box or tower. It holds all the brains of the computer. Then there's the _____________, which is what we look at. There's also the mouse, which is used to tell a computer what to do, and the keyboard, which we _____________ _____________. Those are the _____________, but we can also use a print, a webcam and speakers.

Key Words basics/ parts/ type/ to/ monitor/ use

Respond to Questions

Respond to the following questions. (21-5)

Q1 How long do you use a computer each day?

A1   I use a computer about _________________________ hours per day.

Q2 How many computers are there in your home?

A2   There _________________________ .

Q3 What is your favorite website?

A3   I really like _________________________ .

Q4 What is better, a laptop or a desktop?

A4   I like _________________ because _________________ .

Q5 How fast can you type?

A5   I can type _________________________ words per minute.

Q6 Do you use email?

A6   _________________________ .

Q7 Do you know anyone who uses a computer too much?

A7   Yes. _________________ plays games _________________ hours a day.

Q8 What kinds of jobs need computers?

A8   I think _________________________ needs a computer,
but especially _________________ .

Q9 When you buy a computer, what's the most important thing?

A9   I think _________________ is important.

Q10 What happens if you use a computer too much?

A10   _________________________ .

Personal Experience & Opinion

Question What do you usually do online?

Sample Answer

I do many different things online. Sometimes I play games with friends in different countries. I especially like chess. Sometimes I watch television programs online. I also really like video sites like YouTube. There are so many funny things to watch. I also like to just surf the Internet and find cool stuff and then share it with my friends. I use Facebook sometimes. It's how my friends and I connect with each other. We don't even really use email very much anymore.

My Answer

- I ____ online.
- I also like to ____.
- I use ____.
- It's how ____.

More Questions

1 What computer games are popular in your country?

2 How can computers help us study English?

3 What are some of the bad effects of computers?

Word especially   surf   stuff   connect

Hotels

Word Pronunciation

Listen to the following words and repeat them. ▌22-1▐

□ **suitcase** [sjúːtkèis] *n.* _______________

□ **maid** [méid] *n.* _______________

□ **luxury** [lʌ́kʃəri] *n.* _______________

□ **valet** [vǽlit] *n.* _______________

□ **bellhop** [bélhàp] *n.* _______________

□ **double** [dʌ́bl] *n.* _______________

□ **penthouse** [pénthàus] *n.* _______________

□ **room service** *n.* _______________

□ **lobby** [lábi] *n.* _______________

□ **single** [síŋgl] *n.* _______________

□ **service** [sə́ːrvis] *n.* _______________

□ **doorman** [dɔ́ːrmæ̀n] *n.* _______________

□ **reception** [risépʃən] *n.* _______________

□ **motel** [moutél] *n.* _______________

□ **facility** [fəsíləti] *n.* _______________

Describe Two Pictures 

Look at the pictures and fill in the blanks with the most suitable words. 22-2

1

A man with a ______________ is walking through a hotel ______________.

2

A ______________ is ______________ a hotel room.

Situational Conversation

Listen to the conversation and answer the questions. 22-3

Q1 What kind of room is available?

Q2 How much is a room per night?

Q3 How many nights will the man stay?

Read Aloud

1 **Read the words aloud.** (22-4)

luxury	excellent	valet
arrive	doorman	the reception desk
during your stay	the front desk	arrange

2 **Read the passage aloud.** (22-4)

Luxury hotels / have excellent service. / There is usually / a valet / who will park your car / when you arrive. / Then / there is a doorman / who will welcome you / and open the door. / Inside, / a bellboy / will take your bags / to your room / and the person at the reception desk / will help you / check in / and give you your keys. / If you need anything / during your stay, / you can call the front desk / and they will arrange for you / to have it.

3 **Read the passage and fill in the blanks with the key words.** (22-4)

Hotels come in _________ different _________ and prices. Five star hotels are very expensive. They are usually _________ wonderful places like downtown or on the beach. They have every kind of service and _________ that you can imagine. There are also budget hotels. These are very simple, quite cheap, not very big, and not always in a great location. Most hotels, however, are right in the _________. They are _________ expensive nor _________ and they _________ _________ _________.

Key Words service/ located/ offer/ luxury/ middle/ neither/ cheap/ nice/ styles/ many

Respond to Questions

Respond to the following questions. (22-5)

Q1 How often do you stay in a hotel?

A1　Probably ________________________________ a year.

Q2 How big was the biggest hotel that you have stayed in?

A2　It was ________________________________ stories high.

Q3 Have you ever seen a hotel penthouse?

A3　Yes. It was very ________________________________ .

Q4 How much does a regular hotel room cost in your city?

A4　About ________________________________ per night.

Q5 What do you think of hotel restaurants?

A5　They are usually ________________________________ .

Q6 What is a motel?

A6　A motel is a small hotel, ________________________________ than a hotel.

Q7 What is usually provided in a hotel room?

A7　They usually have ________________________________ .

Q8 Would you like to live in a hotel?

A8　________________________________ .

Q9 What facilities do you like in a hotel?

A9　I like ________________________________ .

Q10 In your country, do you tip the maid?

A10　________________________________ .

Personal Experience & Opinion

Read the question and write your own answer. (22-6)

Question What is your best hotel experience?

Sample Answer

My family and I once took a vacation to Hong Kong. We stayed in a big hotel there. From the window, we could see the entire city. It looked especially nice at night with all the lights of the other buildings. Everyone in the hotel was very nice. The rooms were very big and the beds were very comfortable. My brother and I didn't really want to leave the hotel. My parents even let us order room service once just for fun.

My Answer

- Once I took a vacation to ______________________________.
- I stayed in a ______________________________.
- From the window, I could see ______________________________.
- My favorite part about the hotel was ______________________________.

More Questions

1 What is your worst hotel experience?

2 Describe a famous hotel in your hometown.

3 If you won three nights in a hotel anywhere in the world, where would you go?

Chapter 23

Company

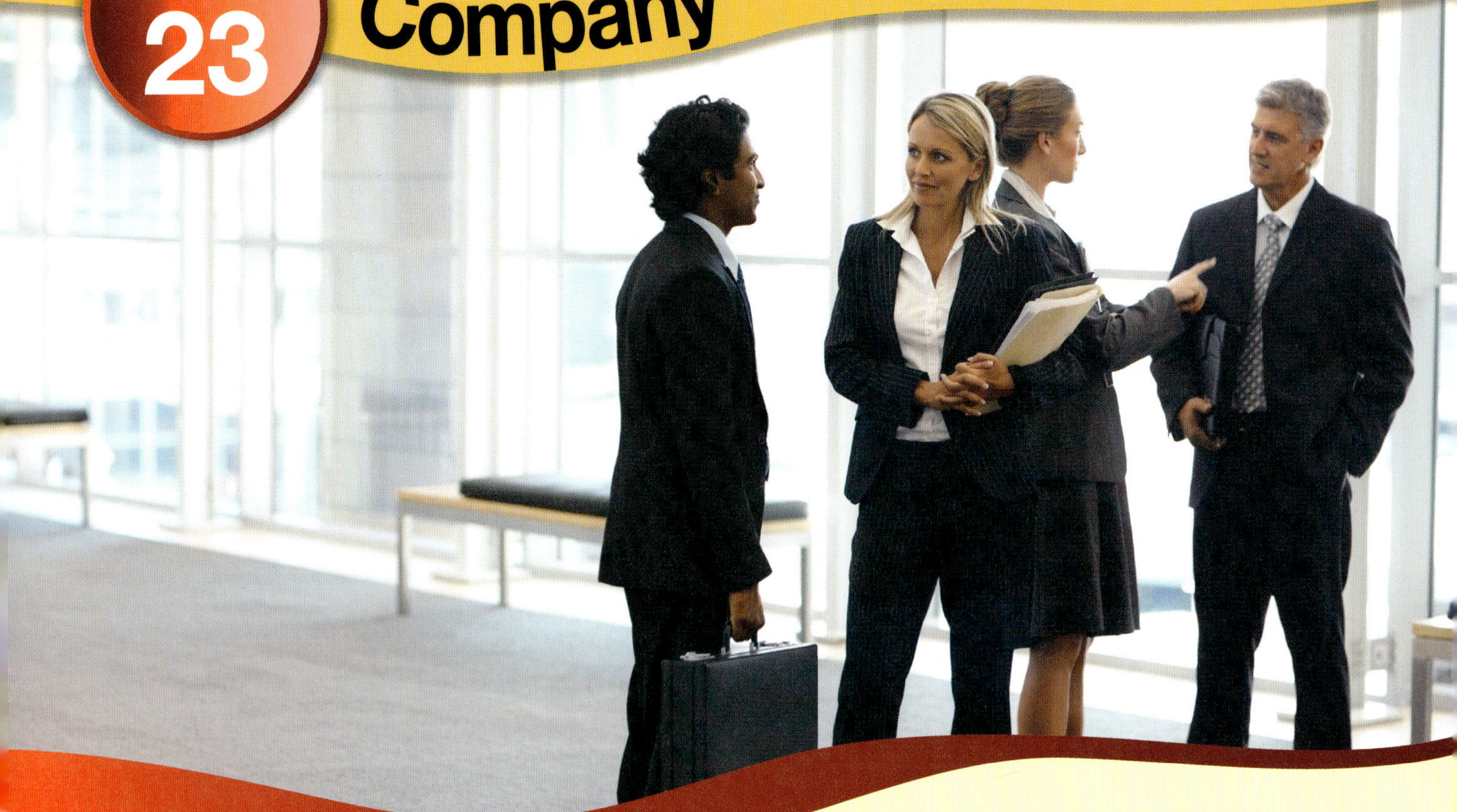

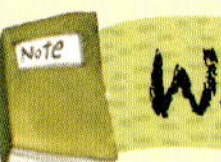

Word Pronunciation

Listen to the following words and repeat them. 23-1

- □ **secretary** [sékrətèri] *n.* ______________
- □ **staff** [stæf] *n.* ______________
- □ **meeting** [mí:tiŋ] *n.* ______________
- □ **fired** [fáiərd] *a.* ______________
- □ **position** [pəzíʃən] *n.* ______________
- □ **employee** [implɔ́ii:] *n.* ______________
- □ **suit** [sú:t] *n.* ______________
- □ **co-worker** *n.* ______________
- □ **telephone** [téləfòun] *n.* ______________
- □ **board room** *n.* ______________
- □ **memo** [mémou] *n.* ______________
- □ **CEO** *n.* ______________
- □ **manager** [mǽnidʒər] *n.* ______________
- □ **retire** [ritáiər] *v.* ______________
- □ **money** [mʌ́ni] *n.* ______________

Describe Two Pictures 

Look at the pictures and fill in the blanks with the most suitable words. 23-2

1

A secretary is ______________ on the ______________.

2

People are having a staff ______________ in a board ______________.

Listen to the conversation and answer the questions. (23-3)

Q1 What happened to Felix?

Q2 What does the man say about Felix?

Q3 Who do you think Mr. Baxter is?

Read Aloud

1 Read the words aloud. (23-4)

position	at the top of	CEO
CFO	organize	everybody's work
adventure	senior manager	employee

2 Read the passage aloud. (23-4)

In any company, / there are / different positions, or jobs. / The CEO / is at the top / of the company. / There might / also be a CFO, / who controls the money, / and a COO, / who organizes everybody's work. / Below these officers / are other important senior managers. / Below them are / middle managers, / who control the work / of all the general employees.

3 Read the passage and fill in the blanks with the key words. (23-4)

Most company offices ______________ ______________ ______________. At the front there is a reception desk where a ______________ or receptionist works. ______________, there is often a big open space with many desks or cubicles, where ______________ ______________ the people in the company work. Around the outside there are closed offices for managers and senior people in the company. We can see this style of office in many movies and TV programs.

Key Words similar/ inside/ look/ of/ most/ quite/ secretary

Respond to Questions

Respond to the following questions. (23-5)

Q1 What is the most famous company in your country?

A1 The most famous company in my country is probably _________________.

Q2 Do you want a fun job or a well-paying job?

A2 I want _________________.

Q3 When do people usually retire in your country?

A3 They usually retire at age _________________.

Q4 What do office workers usually wear to work?

A4 They wear _________________.

Q5 How many hours per week do most people work?

A5 Most work _________________ hours per week.

Q6 What kind of personality should a boss have?

A6 A good boss should be _________________.

Q7 What is your ideal job?

A7 I really want to _________________.

Q8 What do you need to get a good job?

A8 I need _________________.

Q9 Do you think you will need English for work?

A9 _________________.

Q10 What is the most difficult job in a company?

A10 I think _________________ is most difficult.

Personal Experience & Opinion

Read the question and write your own answer. (23-6)

Question   What are the important things to look for in a job?

Sample Answer

There are many things to think about when you look for a job. One of them is money. We need money to able to live, and work is how we get it. Another is happiness. If you don't like your job, you will not be a happy person. Another one is co-workers. We spend so much time at work that we should really like the people we work with. And I guess we should also think about location. I don't want to travel far to go to my office.

My Answer

- When you look for a job, one thing to think about is ________________________.
- We need ________________ to ________________.
- Another one is ________________________________.
- And we should also think about ________________________.

More Questions

1   What are the most popular jobs in your country?

2   If you could work for any company, which one would you choose?

3   Do you want to have one job for your whole life or change jobs?

Word   **guess   location   choose**

Elevator

Word Pronunciation

Listen to the following words and repeat them. (24-1)

- **crowded** [kráudid] *a.* _______________
- **out of order** *a.* _______________
- **shaft** [ʃǽft] *n.* _______________
- **automatic** [ɔ̀:təmǽtik] *a.* _______________
- **press** [prés] *v.* _______________
- **department store** *n.* _______________
- **wait** [wéit] *v.* _______________
- **to make matters worse** *ph.* _______________

- **floor** [flɔ́:r] *n.* _______________
- **machine** [məʃí:n] *n.* _______________
- **constantly** [kánstəntli] *ad.* _______________
- **emergency** [imə́:rdʒənsi] *n.* _______________
- **afraid** [əfréid] *a.* _______________
- **stop** [stáp] *v.* _______________
- **restroom** [réstrùm] *n.* _______________

Describe Two Pictures 

Look at the pictures and fill in the blanks with the most suitable words. (24-2)

1

A group of people are ______________ into an ______________.

2

A woman is pushing the ______________ for ______________ 25.

Situational Conversation

Listen to the conversation and answer the questions. (24-3)

Q1 Where is the woman going?

Q2 How long did the woman have to wait?

Q3 What does the man say about another elevator?

Read Aloud

1 **Read the words aloud.** (❙24-4❙)

one kind of	move	a long shaft
up and down	several	constantly
from floor to floor	a long time	get to the top

2 **Read the passage aloud.** (❙24-4❙)

Elevators are / one kind of machine / that moves people / in buildings. / It is / a box / in a long shaft / that moves up and down / inside a building. / Large buildings / have / several elevators. / They are / all constantly / moving up and down / inside the building, / helping people / get from floor to floor. / In a very tall building, / the elevator / can take a long time / to get to the top!

3 **Read the passage and fill in the blanks with the key words.** (❙24-4❙)

When elevators _____________ first _______________, there was a special person in a uniform who opened the doors and _______________ the buttons. Now, the doors are _______________ and we push our own buttons. There is usually a button for each story of the building. There is also one to hold the door open and one to close the door. There is also an _______________ button that we can press if something _______________ happens.

Key Words bad/ emergency/ automatic/ invented/ were/ pushed

Respond to Questions

Respond to the following questions. (24-5)

Q1 Where do you usually take the elevator?
A1   I take an elevator in ________________________ .

Q2 Do you know anyone who is afraid of elevators?
A2   Yes. ________________________ is afraid of elevators.

Q3 What's the longest elevator ride you have taken?
A3   I took an elevator to the top of an ________________ -story building.

Q4 If the elevator is broken, what can you do?
A4   I can ________________________ .

Q5 When should you NOT use the elevator?
A5   If there is ________________________ , we shouldn't use the elevator.

Q6 What happens if the elevator doors close on you?
A6   ________________________ .

Q7 Do you usually push onto a crowded elevator or wait for the next one?
A7   I usually ________________________ .

Q8 Should people first get on or first get off?
A8   People should ________________________ .

Q9 Have you ever been in a glass elevator?
A9   Yes, it was ________________________ !

Q10 What kind of building usually has large elevators?
A10   ________________________ have large elevators.

Personal Experience & Opinion

Read the question and write your own answer. (24-6)

Question What is the worst experience you've had in an elevator?

Sample Answer

I got stuck in an elevator once. I was going up to the top floor of a department store. There were about 10 people on the elevator. Suddenly, the elevator stopped between the fourth and fifth floors. We had to wait a really long time. It was very hot, and one person was crying. To make matters worse, I really had to go to the restroom!

My Answer

- I ________________________ in an elevator.
- Suddenly, ________________________ .
- We had to ________________________ .
- To make things worse, ________________________ .

More Questions

1 What are some famous buildings where you would like to try the elevators?

2 Besides buildings, what kinds of things use elevators?

3 Describe the nicest elevator you have been in.

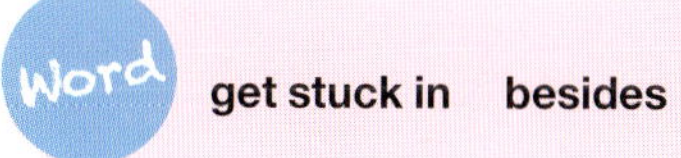

Word get stuck in   besides